Marguerite Patten's
Sunday Lunch Cookbook

Marguerite Patten's Sunday Lunch Cookbook

DAVID & CHARLES
Newton Abbot   London   North Pomfret (Vt)

Frontispiece: Menu 6
Roast Topside of Beef with Yorkshire Pudding, Roast Potatoes, Roast Parsnips; Apple Pie

Acknowledgements
The author and publishers gratefully acknowledge the considerable assistance given by TI Creda Ltd and their Home Economist, Margaret Weale, in the preparation of the colour photographs. Josiah Wedgwood and Sons Ltd kindly supplied the dishes used in all the photographs except those on pp 41 and 95 which were supplied by Corning Ltd, makers of Pyrex.

British Library Cataloguing in Publication Data

Patten, Marguerite
    Marguerite Patten's Sunday lunch cookbook.
    1. Luncheons
    I. Title
    641.5'3   TX735

    ISBN 0-7153-8381-7

© Text: Marguerite Patten 1983
© Colour illustrations: TI Creda Ltd 1983
    (except pp 41 and 95)

Typeset by Typesetters (Birmingham) Ltd
and printed in The Netherlands
by Smeets Offset BV, Weert
for David & Charles (Publishers) Limited
Brunel House   Newton Abbot   Devon

Published in the United States of America
by David & Charles Inc
North Pomfret   Vermont 05053   USA

Contents
(Numbers given refer to menus)

Introduction

It has given me great pleasure to compile this *Sunday Lunch Cookbook* for it has offered great scope in the selection of menus and recipes. Sunday is the day when most of us can relax rather more than on other days of the week; it may also be the only day when the immediate family can get together for a home-cooked lunch.

Please do not imagine this is a book based entirely upon good 'old-fashioned' roast joints, once the accepted food for a Sunday lunch. There will be times when you want to cook this enjoyable type of meal, but modern living has changed many established habits. I have therefore planned meals for a variety of occasions, as you will see from the Contents page.

If the family are tired after a busy week, why not have a leisurely morning and combine breakfast and lunch for the informal meal that has been christened 'brunch'? If the sun shines, make the best use of the good weather by planning a picnic, barbecue or meal in the garden. There will be Sundays when you require a lighter meal than usual or, on the other hand, a rather more unusual and elaborate meal for a special celebration. All these are included in the fifty-three menus for I have assumed that Christmas Day could well fall on a Sunday.

The menus are not only planned to cover various situations, but to make the best use of seasonal foods and various parts of the cooker. You will notice that when the oven is required for one dish, I have made sure that other courses also can be cooked in the oven. Each menu starts with a light hors d'oeuvre; you may like to omit this course, although I feel it makes the lunch more interesting. If you do prefer a two-course meal, I think you will find the hors d'oeuvre recipes helpful for another meal.

I wanted the cook to have as leisurely a Sunday as possible, so I have included hints on preparing ahead and freezing, together with a complete list of foods required for each menu. I felt this was more helpful than just a shopping list of perishable foods. The only items omitted from the list are salt, pepper and stock, together with cheeses, if you like to serve cheese after the dessert. Should you have no stock in the refrigerator or freezer, you will sometimes need to add stock cubes to the list of foods needed.

The dishes in the various menus have been planned to please most tastes, from those of young children to more sophisticated palates, for Sunday lunch is a meal to be enjoyed by all the family.

I always look forward to my Sundays when I have my family and friends with me. I hope this book will add to your enjoyment of Sundays.

Marguerite Patten.

Menu 1
Aubergine Salad; Lemon Meringue Pie

6

Choose a really good red wine to accompany this meal. While a Bordeaux would be perfect, these clarets have become expensive, so look for good red wines from the Rhône area such as Châteauneuf du Pape. There are excellent red wines from Spain, especially from the Rioja and Penédes areas.

Aubergine Salad
2 medium aubergines
salt and pepper
2tbspn olive oil
225g (8oz) fresh or frozen
   mange tout peas
4 large tomatoes
lettuce
watercress
4tbspn French Dressing (see
   Menu 34)

Lamb with Ham and Celery Stuffing
small celery heart
50g (2oz) butter
100g (4oz) cooked rice
2tbspn chopped parsley
2tbspn chopped chives
100g (4oz) cooked ham
1 egg
salt and pepper
1 boned leg of lamb

Potatoes Forestière
675g (1½lb) old potatoes
salt and pepper
100g (4oz) mushrooms
50g (2oz) butter or margarine
4tbspn milk

Creamed Spinach
675-900g (1½-2lb) spinach
salt and pepper
25g (1oz) butter or margarine
3tbspn double cream

<table>
<tr><td>Menu 1
Serves 6</td><td>Aubergine Salad

Lamb with Ham and Celery Stuffing
Potatoes Forestière – Creamed Spinach

Lemon Meringue Pie</td></tr>
</table>

Aubergine Salad
Wipe, then score the skin of the aubergines, sprinkle with a little salt, leave for 30 minutes (the salt draws out the bitter taste from the aubergines). Strain away any liquid, rinse the aubergines in cold water, dry well; cut into slices, then quarter each slice. Heat the oil in a frying pan, fry the aubergines until tender, but unbroken. Drain on absorbent paper, allow to cool. Meanwhile, lightly cook and strain the peas; cut the tomatoes into wedges. Prepare the lettuce and watercress, put on to a flat dish. Top with the other ingredients and moisten with well-seasoned French Dressing.

Lamb with Ham and Celery Stuffing
Chop the celery finely. Heat the butter and fry the celery for a few minutes; blend with the rice and herbs. Chop the ham finely, add to the stuffing together with the egg. Season well. Press into the cavity of the lamb, secure with skewers or fine string. Weigh and roast as described on page 10, using Temperature 2.

This particular stuffing is excellent cold, so any lamb left over could be served with a salad.

Potatoes Forestière
Peel the potatoes and cook in boiling salted water until only just tender. Strain and cut into 0.5cm (¼in) slices. Wipe and thinly slice the mushrooms. Put the potatoes and mushrooms into an oven-proof serving dish, beginning and ending with a layer of potatoes. Heat the butter or margarine and milk together, season well; pour over the potatoes. Bake uncovered for 35-40 minutes in a very moderate to moderate oven, 160-180°C, 325-350°F, Gas Mark 3-4.

Creamed Spinach
Wash the spinach in several lots of cold water. Put into a saucepan and cook in the water adhering to the leaves. Add a little salt only. Strain well, then chop very finely. Return to the pan with the butter or margarine, cream, and salt and pepper to taste. Heat thoroughly.

Lemon Meringue Pie
This method of baking the pie is excellent whether you are serving it hot or cold. If you intend to serve it hot, prepare earlier and just put back into a cool oven when serving the first course of the meal; in this way there is no fear of the pastry or filling being over-cooked as so often happens when trying to cook with a roast joint (see also Variation).

Sift the flour and salt into a mixing bowl, rub in the butter or margarine, add the sugar and water to bind. Roll out and line a 20cm (8in) deep flan dish or tin or a 23cm (9in) more shallow container. Bake 'blind' as described in Menu 26 until crisp and pale golden; do not over-cook. Blend the cornflour with the water, lemon rind and juice. Put into a saucepan with the butter and 75g (3oz) sugar and stir over a low heat until thickened and smooth. Remove from the heat. Separate the eggs, whisk the yolks into the lemon mixture. Return to the heat and cook gently, stirring all the time, for 2-3 minutes until a very thick mixture once again. Spoon into the pastry case. Whisk the egg whites until very stiff; gradually beat in 75g (3oz) sugar, fold in the remaining 75g (3oz). Spoon on top of the lemon filling. Make sure the meringue touches the sides and top of the pastry and there is no gap between the pastry and the lemon mixture. If there is a gap it causes moisture to form. Return to a cool oven, lowering the heat to 140°C, 275°F, Gas Mark 1, and set for 1½ hours. By cooking in this manner and using a high percentage of sugar, the meringue stays crisp when cold.

To Make Sunday Easier

1 Make French Dressing (see Menu 34) for hors d'oeuvre when convenient; store in screw-topped jar.
2 Stuff meat ready for roasting. Make stock from bone for gravy.
3 Cook potatoes, but do not prepare complete dish; this becomes over-soft if you do.
4 Bake pie if having this cold. If serving hot, line the dish with the pastry; cover well and put in refrigerator. Make the filling and keep in a covered container. Put into the pastry on Sunday and proceed as recipe.

Foods Required

Boned leg of lamb (give butcher adequate notice about boning meat or see remarks below), 100g (4oz) cooked ham, 240g (9½oz) butter or margarine, 3tbspn double cream, 4 eggs, 4tbspn milk, 2tbspn olive oil plus oil and vinegar or lemon juice for French Dressing (see Menu 34), 50g (2oz) rice (you need 100g (4oz) when cooked), 175g (6oz) flour (preferably plain), 25g (1oz) cornflour, 275g (10oz) caster sugar plus little for dressing, 225g (8oz) fresh or frozen mange tout peas, 4 large tomatoes, 2 medium aubergines, lettuce, watercress, small celery heart, parsley, few chives, 675g (1½lb) old potatoes, 100g (4oz) mushrooms, 675-900g (1½-2lb) spinach, 3 lemons.

Boning Meat and Poultry

It is not difficult to bone meat or poultry, but it takes time and patience. You need a sharp and flexible knife so that you can cut around the shaped bone or bones. First, make a firm downwards cut into the flesh until you feel the bone, then change the angle of the knife and slowly and carefully cut the meat away from the bone; eventually, you will be able to remove the bone entirely.

Lemon Meringue Pie

For the sweet shortcrust pastry
175g (6oz) flour (preferably plain)
pinch salt
90g (3½oz) butter or margarine
25g (1oz) caster sugar
water to bind

For the filling and topping
25g (1oz) cornflour
300ml (½pt) water
2tspn very finely grated lemon rind ('zest')
6tbspn lemon juice
25g (1oz) butter
250g (9oz) caster sugar
3 eggs

Variation
If you dislike such a sweet meringue, then allow only 75g (3oz) sugar to 3 egg whites. You can then brown the meringue and set it lightly in a very moderate oven, 160°C, 325°F, Gas Mark 3, for 20 minutes or a slightly longer time at a lower setting. This meringue is not crisp when cold.

To Freeze Ahead

Stuffing freezes well except that the celery becomes watery and limp; this vegetable could be added to the other ingredients after defrosting.
Pastry for Lemon Meringue Pie or cooked pastry shell could be frozen; this is more satisfactory than freezing completed pie.

Making Gravy

People vary in the amount of gravy they like, but it is far better to make too much rather than too little. 600ml (1pt) would make generous portions for 6 people.

For a thin gravy

Pour all the dripping (fat) from the roasting tin except 1½tbspn. Leave in all those delicious little pieces of meat and stuffing that fall into the tin — these add flavour. If you prefer, spoon the 1½tbspn dripping, plus any residue from the roasting tin, into a saucepan. Blend 2 level tbspn flour into the fat; stir over a low heat until the flour turns a nutty brown colour. You can add a little gravy browning for extra colour. Gradually blend in 600ml (1pt) well-strained vegetable stock or stock from bones, poultry or game giblets. Stir as the liquid comes to the boil, taste the gravy and adjust the seasoning; add any flavourings (see below). Strain into a heated sauce boat or keep hot until ready to serve.

For a thicker gravy

Use 40g (1½oz) flour to the proportions of dripping and liquid above. This recipe is for a good basic gravy; you can add your own favourite flavourings or as suggested below.

Additional flavourings

Add 1-2tbspn port wine or red or white wine (depending on the food with which it is served).

Add a little mushroom ketchup or garlic salt or Worcestershire or soy sauce.

Roasting Meat, Poultry and Game

Read the instructions in the recipes for the method of preparing each type of meat, poultry or game.

Always calculate the cooking time *after* stuffing the joint or bird.

Two temperatures are given, No 1 and No 2. No 1 is for a moderately hot to hot oven and is therefore suitable for prime fresh meat.

Temperature 2, which is very moderate to moderate, is the one to choose for defrosted poultry or for defrosted meat or the less expensive cuts. If more convenient, you could select this lower temperature for all poultry and all meat, but I would *not* advise using Temperature 1 for any defrosted poultry or meat if you want it really tender.

You will notice I have given a slight range of settings in both Temperatures 1 and 2; this is because individual ovens vary a great deal. If you consider your oven slower than average, then use the higher setting; if, on the other hand, you think it is rather hotter than average, then use the lower one.

Temperature 1 — Higher Heat

Set the oven to 200-220°C, 400-425°F, Gas Mark 6-7. After cooking the poultry or a joint for 1 hour, reduce the heat to 190°-200°C, 375-400°F, Gas Mark 5-6.

The list below gives times to allow:

Poultry and Young Game Birds
15 minutes per 450g (1lb) and 15 minutes over, up to 5.4kg (12lb), then 12 minutes per *additional* 450g (1lb).

Beef
Rare: 15 minutes per 450g (1lb) and 15 minutes over.
Medium: 20 minutes per 450g (1lb) and 20 minutes over.

Lamb
20 minutes per 450g (1lb) and 20 minutes over.

Pork, Veal and Venison
25 minutes per 450g (1lb) and 25 minutes over.

Temperature 2 — Lower Heat

Set the oven to 160-180°C, 325-350°F, Gas Mark 3-4. Keep at this temperature throughout the cooking period.

The list below gives times to allow:

Poultry and Young Game Birds
22-25 minutes per 450g (1lb) and 22-25 minutes over, up to 5.4kg (12lb), then 20 minutes per *additional* 450g (1lb).

Beef
Rare: 25 minutes per 450g (1lb) and 25 minutes over.
Medium: 30 minutes per 450g (1lb) and 30 minutes over.

Lamb
35 minutes per 450g (1lb) and 35 minutes over.

Pork, Veal and Venison
40 minutes per 450g (1lb) and 40 minutes over.

If using a covered roasting tin, allow an extra 10 minutes. If wrapping the bird or meat in foil, allow an extra 15-20 minutes cooking time. No extra time is required if using a roaster bag.

<table>
<tr><td>

Menu 2

Serves 4

</td><td>

Baked Eggs Benedictine

Kidneys Turbigo with Rice and Courgettes

Cheese and Biscuits – Fresh Fruit

</td></tr>
</table>

Baked Eggs Benedictine

Wipe the mushrooms, slice very thinly. Heat half the butter in a pan, cook the mushrooms until just soft. Peel the garlic clove; either crush this or put through a garlic press to extract juice; blend the garlic or garlic juice with the cream, the cooked mushrooms, salt and pepper to taste. Butter 4 small ramekin dishes; melt the remaining butter. Break an egg into each dish, season lightly, top with the melted butter, then the cream mixture. Bake towards the top of a moderately hot oven, 200°C, 400°F, Gas Mark 6, for 8-10 minutes until the eggs are just set. Garnish with paprika and serve with a teaspoon.

Crisp brown toast is a good accompaniment.

Kidneys Turbigo

Halve and skin the kidneys, cut away any excess fat. Blend the flour with a little salt and pepper. Coat the kidneys in the seasoned flour Heat 50g (2oz) butter in a deep frying pan. Fry the kidneys for 10 minutes or until tender, then remove from the pan on to a heated dish. Meanwhile, wipe the mushrooms, add the remaining butter to the pan and fry the mushrooms and sausages until tender. Arrange on the dish with the kidneys. Pour the stock and wine into the pan, stir well to absorb any fat that remains. Cook until slightly thickened, then add salt, pepper and mustard to taste. Spoon over the kidney mixture and top with parsley.

Serve with Rice (see Menu 32) and Courgettes (see Menu 23).

Cheese and Biscuits

Serve the cheese with crisp celery. As the kidney dish has a very definite flavour, it is wise to choose a cheese that has a pronounced taste.

Fresh Fruit

These three fruits give a pleasing contrast in colour on a fruit dish.

To Make Sunday Easier

1 Prepare base of Baked Eggs Benedictine; add eggs before cooking.
2 Prepare kidney dish if not freezing this.

Foods Required

8 lambs' kidneys, 8 small sausages or Frankfurters, 115g (4½oz) butter, selection of cheeses (see menu), 6tbspn double cream, 4 eggs, 15g (½oz) flour, 175-225g (6-8oz) long grain rice, mustard or paprika, 4tbspn red or port wine (see Kidneys Turbigo), 175g (6oz) mushrooms (or see Variation under Kidneys Turbigo), garlic clove (optional), parsley, 450-675g (1-1½lb) courgettes, fruit (see menu).

A kidney dish needs a robust red wine. Try a Californian red wine – not cheap, but excellent.

Baked Eggs Benedictine

50g (2oz) mushrooms
40g (1½oz) butter
1 garlic clove (optional)
6tbspn double cream
salt and pepper
4 eggs

To garnish
paprika

Kidneys Turbigo

8 lambs' kidneys
15g (½oz) flour
salt and pepper
75g (3oz) butter
100g (4oz) button mushrooms
8 small sausages or Frankfurters
150ml (¼pt) chicken stock
4tbspn red or port wine or extra stock
½-1tspn made mustard

To garnish
1tbspn chopped parsley

Variation
Omit mushrooms as they are already in first course.

Rice and Courgettes

175-225g (6-8oz) long grain rice
450-675g (1-1½lb) courgettes
salt

Cheese and Biscuits

Suggested cheeses
Danish Blue
Lancashire
Sage Derby

Fresh Fruit

crisp dessert apples
grapes
tangerines

To Freeze Ahead

Fried mushrooms freeze well. Kidneys Turbigo freeze well for several weeks. Rice can be frozen (see Menu 8).

Serve a chilled dry sherry with the hors d'oeuvre and a robust red wine such as Hermitage or a Hungarian red with the casserole.

Menu 3	Avocados en Cocotte
Serves 6	Pheasant Casserole
	Jacket Potatoes
	Carrot Casserole – Russian-style Cabbage
	Orange Chiffon Pie

Avocados en Cocotte

For the filling
3 eggs
75g (3oz) cooked ham or salami
50g (2oz) butter
2tbspn mayonnaise (see Menu 34) or double cream
3tbspn soft breadcrumbs
salt and cayenne pepper
pinch mustard powder

3 ripe avocados
2tbspn lemon juice

For the topping
25g (1oz) butter
3tbspn soft breadcrumbs
3tbspn grated cheese

Pheasant Casserole

2 small pheasants
salt and pepper
bouquet garni
450ml (¾pt) stock (see method)
225g (8oz) chestnuts
25g (1oz) flour
4 thick back bacon rashers
50g (2oz) butter
100g (4oz) mushrooms

To garnish
fried croûtons (see Menu 5)

Variation
Use a little less stock and add red or port wine to the sauce.

Jacket Potatoes

6 medium potatoes
40g (1½oz) butter

Carrot Casserole

550g (1¼lb) carrots
1 medium onion
salt and pepper
knob of butter

Avocados en Cocotte

Hard-boil, shell and chop the eggs. Finely chop the ham or salami, melt the butter. Mix the eggs, ham or salami and butter with the remaining ingredients for the filling, blend well until a soft spreading consistency. Halve the avocados, put into a shallow oven-proof serving dish (cut side uppermost) and top with the lemon juice. Spoon the filling over, press down firmly. Melt the butter for the topping and mix with the breadcrumbs and cheese; sprinkle over the filling. Bake just above the centre of a moderate oven, 180°C, 350°F, Gas Mark 4, for 15 minutes until the topping is delicately browned. Do not over-cook as this spoils the flavour of the avocados.

Pheasant Casserole

Cut each pheasant into 4 portions, ie 2 leg joints and 2 breast joints. Put the giblets and rest of the pheasant carcass into a pan, cover with water. Add salt and pepper and bouquet garni. Simmer for about 1 hour, strain. Retain 450ml (¾pt) stock. Slit chestnut skins, put in water to cover, simmer for 10 minutes; remove skins while hot. Season the flour and coat the pheasant joints. Derind and chop the bacon. Heat the butter in a large saucepan, fry the bacon and mushrooms for 2-3 minutes. Remove from the pan and put into a casserole. Place the coated pheasant joints in the remaining butter in the pan, fry until golden brown, then put into the casserole with the chestnuts. Pour the stock into the saucepan, stir well, then spoon over the food in the casserole. Cover tightly. If the pheasants are young and tender, cook for 1¼ hours in the centre of a moderate oven, 180°C, 350°F, Gas Mark 4. If these are older birds, allow 2 hours in a very moderate oven, 160°C, 325°F, Gas Mark 3. Top with croûtons just before serving.

Jacket Potatoes

Scrub the potatoes, dry well. Prick the skins and rub with a buttered paper; this helps the skins to become crisp. Put on to a baking tray. Cook for 1¼ hours towards the top of a moderate oven or a little longer in a very moderate oven. Cut a cross on each potato and top with a knob of butter.

Carrot Casserole

Peel the carrots and cut into long strips. Peel and chop the onion very finely. Put the carrots and onion into a casserole with water to cover and a generous amount of salt and pepper. Cover the casserole. Cook for about 1 hour in the coolest part of a moderate oven or a little longer in a very moderate oven. Strain and toss in a little butter.

Russian-style Cabbage

Peel and finely chop the onion; peel and finely dice the apple(s). Prepare and shred the cabbage very thinly; put into the minimum quantity of boiling salted water and cook for a very few minutes only so it retains a firm texture; strain. Add the butter or margarine to the saucepan, fry the apple(s) and onion for a few minutes; tip the cabbage back into the pan, stir to blend with the apples and onion, heat for about 1 minute.

Orange Chiffon Pie

Crush the biscuits, melt the butter. Blend the biscuit crumbs, butter and sugar together. Press into a 20cm (8in) flan dish. Chill well before filling. Put 4tbspn orange juice into a basin. Add the gelatine, dissolve over hot water. Separate the eggs, whisk the yolks and sugar over hot water until thick and creamy, then whisk in the dissolved gelatine and the remainder of the orange juice. Allow the mixture to cool and begin to stiffen. Whisk the cream until it stands in peaks in one bowl, and the egg whites until very stiff in a second bowl. Fold into the partially set jelly. Spoon into the biscuit crumb crust. Leave until firm. Cut away the peel and pith from the oranges and cut out the orange segments. Moisten the angelica and cut into leaf shapes. Arrange the orange segments and angelica on top of the jelly.

To Make Sunday Easier

1 Avocados should not be cut until just before serving or cooking. The filling could be prepared ahead, covered and put in the refrigerator.
2 Cook Pheasant Casserole if not freezing this; the flavour of this, like most casseroles, is improved by cooking, then cooling the dish and storing it in the refrigerator for 24 hours.
3 Make Orange Chiffon Pie; add decoration just before serving.

Foods Required

2 small pheasants, 4 thick back bacon rashers, 75g (3oz) cooked ham or salami, 240-265g (9½-10½oz) butter plus extra if using this to fry croûtons, also butter for Carrot Casserole, fat or oil if not using butter for croûtons, 3tbspn grated Cheddar or other hard cheese, 150ml (¼pt) double cream plus 2tbspn if not using mayonnaise in avocado filling, 5 eggs, 25g (1oz) flour, bread to give 6tbspn crumbs plus amount for croûtons, 2tbspn mayonnaise (see Menu 34) if not using cream in avocado filling, 175g (6oz) digestive biscuits, 100g (4oz) caster sugar, 15g (½oz) gelatine, 200ml (7½fl oz) orange juice, piece angelica, cayenne pepper, mustard, 6 medium potatoes, 550g (1¼lb) carrots, 2 onions, 225g (8oz) chestnuts, 100g (4oz) mushrooms, 1 small red or green cabbage, mixed herbs (bouquet garni), 3 avocados, 1 lemon (to give 2tbspn juice), 2 oranges (unless using fresh oranges to give orange juice, then 4-5 required), 1 to 2 dessert apples.

Russian-style Cabbage

1 small onion
1 or 2 dessert apples
1 small red or green cabbage
salt
25-50g (1-2oz) butter or
    margarine

Variations
1 Cook the cabbage in one pan and the onion and apples in a second pan so the cabbage is not kept waiting.
2 Add ½-1tspn carraway seeds to the cabbage while it is cooking.

Orange Chiffon Pie

For the biscuit crust
175g (6oz) digestive biscuits
50g (2oz) butter
50g (2oz) caster sugar

For the filling
200ml (7½fl oz) orange juice
15g (½oz) gelatine
2 eggs
50g (2oz) caster sugar
150ml (¼pt) double cream

To decorate
2 oranges
angelica

To Freeze Ahead

Avocados en Cocotte cannot be frozen.
Pheasant Casserole freezes well; this dish is excellent made with defrosted frozen pheasants.
Croûtons: open-freeze, then pack.
Orange Chiffon Pie freezes well; add fresh orange segments after defrosting. Always allow a mixture containing gelatine to set completely before freezing.

A young red Burgundy or a slightly sweet white wine would be a good choice to serve with the bacon.

Leek Soup
450g (1lb) leeks
40g (1½oz) butter
600ml (1pt) chicken stock
salt and pepper
little double cream (optional)
chopped chives and parsley

Grilled Bacon with Cumberland Sauce

For the Cumberland Sauce
2 large oranges
300ml (½pt) water
2tspn arrowroot or cornflour
2tbspn port wine
1tbspn lemon juice
1-2tspn made English or
    French mustard
4tbspn redcurrant jelly
salt and pepper

4 thick back rashers (bacon
    chops)
100-175g (4-6oz) button
    mushrooms
4 orange slices

Chocolate Chip Pudding
110g (4oz) butter or margarine
110g (4oz) caster sugar
2 eggs
150g (5oz) self-raising flour or
    plain flour with 1¼tspn
    baking powder
2tbspn milk
75g (3oz) plain chocolate

For the Coffee Sauce
1½tbspn cornflour
150ml (¼pt) strong coffee
300ml (½pt) milk
50g (2oz) caster sugar

To Freeze Ahead
Leek Soup freezes excellently; add cream after defrosting. Cumberland Sauce freezes well. Chocolate Chip Pudding can be frozen for up to 3 months.

Menu 4	Leek Soup
Serves 4	Grilled Bacon with Cumberland Sauce
	Creamed Potatoes – Brussels Sprouts
	Chocolate Chip Pudding and Coffee Sauce

Leek Soup
Wash and chop the leeks; avoid any tough green parts. Heat the butter in a saucepan, put in the leeks, heat for 2-3 minutes; do not allow to brown. Add the stock, salt and pepper. Cook for about 10 minutes only to preserve the delicate colour of the leeks. Sieve or liquidise to give a smooth purée. Reheat or serve cold. Top with cream and herbs.

Grilled Bacon with Cumberland Sauce
Remove the top orange part of the rind (the 'zest') from 1 orange and cut into thin matchstick pieces. Put into the water; allow to stand for 1 hour if possible. Simmer for 15 minutes, or until the peel is tender and the liquid reduced to 150ml (¼pt). Halve both oranges, squeeze out the juice. Blend the arrowroot or cornflour with the port wine, add to the liquid in the pan with the fruit juices, mustard, jelly, a little salt and pepper. Stir over a low heat until thickened and smooth. Serve hot.

    Meanwhile, remove the rind from the bacon, snip the fat, grill the chops on either side until golden; lower the heat and cook until tender. Wipe the mushrooms, brush with a little bacon fat, cook under the grill for 5 minutes. Serve round the chops. Top with orange slices.

    For Creamed Potatoes, see Menu 7; Brussels Sprouts, see Menu 6.

Chocolate Chip Pudding and Coffee Sauce
Cream together the butter or margarine and sugar. Gradually beat in the eggs. Sift the flour, or flour and baking powder. Fold into the creamed mixture together with the milk. Chop the chocolate, add to the sponge. Spoon into a greased 1 litre (1¾pt) basin. Cover and steam for 1½ hours. Turn out and serve with Coffee Sauce. Blend the cornflour with the cold coffee. Heat the milk and sugar, pour over the blended mixture. Return to the saucepan; stir over a low heat until thickened.

To Make Sunday Easier
1   Prepare soup ahead unless freezing this.
2   Make Cumberland Sauce unless freezing this.
3   Make pudding; store in refrigerator unless freezing this.

Foods Required
4 thick back rashers (bacon chops), 175-200g (6½-7½oz) butter, little double cream (if adding to soup), 2 eggs, 450ml (¾pt) milk, 150g (5oz) self-raising flour or plain flour with 1¼tspn baking powder, 160g (6oz) caster sugar, 1½tbspn cornflour, 2tspn arrowroot or cornflour, 2tbspn port wine, English or French mustard, 4tbspn redcurrant jelly, 75g (3oz) plain chocolate, instant coffee to make 450ml (¾pt), 450g (1lb) leeks, 100-175g (4-6oz) button mushrooms, 450-675g (1-1½lb) sprouts, 450-675g (1-1½lb) potatoes, parsley, chives, 3 oranges, 1 lemon.

Menu 4
Leek Soup; Grilled Bacon with Cumberland Sauce, Creamed Potatoes, Brussels Sprouts

A good full-bodied red wine is the ideal choice for the main dish. Choose a Burgundy or good Spanish red wine.

Menu 5

Serves 6

Avocado and Orange Salad

Jugged Hare with Forcemeat Balls,
Fried Croûtons and Redcurrant Jelly
Parsley Potatoes — Red Cabbage

Viennoise Pudding

Avocado and Orange Salad

2tbspn salad oil
1tbspn lemon juice
1tbspn orange juice
salt and pepper
2 large oranges
2 medium avocados
lettuce

Jugged Hare

1 jointed hare with blood and
   liver
900ml (1½pt) water
2tbspn vinegar
salt and pepper
50g (2oz) flour
2 medium onions
2 medium carrots
75g (3oz) dripping or fat
150ml (¼pt) red or port wine
2tbspn redcurrant jelly

To garnish
Forcemeat Balls
Fried Croûtons

Forcemeat Balls

100g (4oz) soft breadcrumbs
50g (2oz) shredded suet
2tbspn chopped parsley
1tspn grated lemon rind
1tbspn lemon juice
½tspn chopped fresh or good
   pinch dried thyme
1 egg yolk
salt and pepper

Fried Croûtons

2-3 slices of bread
50-75g (2-3oz) butter or
   2-3tbspn oil

Variations
1 Croûtons can be deep fried.
2 Cut very small dice to serve
with soup, then fry.

Avocado and Orange Salad

Blend together the oil, lemon and orange juice, salt and pepper to taste. Cut away the peel from the oranges and cut the fruit into segments. Halve and skin the avocados and put immediately into the dressing. Add the orange segments. Prepare the lettuce; shred and put into individual dishes. Top with the avocado and orange mixture.

Jugged Hare

Put the blood of the hare on one side. Place the liver in a pan with the water. Cover the pan and simmer for 45 minutes or until the liver is tender. Strain the liquid, add more water to make 900ml (1½pt) once again. Meanwhile, soak the hare for 1 hour in cold water with the vinegar. Drain and dry on absorbent paper. Season the flour and coat the joints with half of this. Peel and slice the onions and carrots. Heat the dripping or fat in a large saucepan. Fry the joints of hare until just golden. Remove from the pan, then fry the onions and carrots for a few minutes. Lift these out of the saucepan. Stir in the remaining flour, then blend in the 900ml (1½pt) stock. Bring to the boil, add the wine, blood of the hare and redcurrant jelly. Sieve or mash the liver, stir into the sauce and season well. The liver adds a delicious flavour and texture to this sauce. Replace the hare, onions and carrots into the sauce. Simmer for 2½-3 hours on top of the cooker or transfer to a casserole and cook for 3 hours in the centre of a slow oven, 150°C, 300°F, Gas Mark 2. Garnish with the Forcemeat Balls and Croûtons. Serve with redcurrant jelly.

For Parsley Potatoes and Red Cabbage, see Menus 3, 7 and 43.

Forcemeat Balls

Mix all the ingredients together. Form into about 12 small balls. If the mixture is slightly crumbly, moisten your fingers before handling. Put on to an oven-proof dish. Bake for 20-25 minutes in a moderately hot oven, 190-200°C, 375-400°F, Gas Mark 5-6. These will need to be cooked earlier if the oven is set at slow for the Jugged Hare, then reheated for a few minutes before serving the meal.

Fried Croûtons

Cut the bread into neat shapes; croûtons for Jugged Hare are often cut into heart shapes. Heat the butter or oil in a frying pan and fry the bread until crisp and brown on either side. Drain on absorbent paper.

Viennoise Pudding

Put the sugar and water into a heavy pan. Stir until the sugar has dissolved, then boil steadily until a dark-coloured caramel. Take the pan off the heat, allow the caramel to cool slightly, then add the milk and cream. Heat gently over a low heat until the milk has absorbed the caramel. Do not allow the mixture to boil as it will curdle. Dice the bread, put into a basin. Pour the warm caramel liquid over this. Allow to soak for at least 30 minutes. Chop the cherries, peel and nuts; beat the eggs well. Add to the caramel mixture together with the other ingredients. Grease a 1.2 litre (2pt) basin or soufflé dish, pour in the mixture. Cover with greased greaseproof paper or foil. Steam gently *without boiling* for approximately 2½ hours, or bake uncovered in a bain-marie in the centre of a slow oven for approximately 1¾ hours. Serve hot with cream or ice-cream.

To Make Sunday Easier

1 Prepare and cook the Jugged Hare unless this is being frozen; cool and store overnight in the refrigerator. The flavour is improved by standing for 24 hours.
2 The Forcemeat Balls and Croûtons can be cooked ready for reheating in the oven on two flat plates or dishes.
3 Prepare the Viennoise Pudding; it can be pre-cooked and heated gently over hot, but not boiling, water or the pudding can be mixed, put into the basin or soufflé dish and kept overnight in the refrigerator ready to cook on Sunday.

Foods Required

Jointed hare, complete with blood and liver, 50-75g (2-3oz) butter (or extra oil), 75g (3oz) dripping or fat, 50g (2oz) shredded suet, 300ml (½pt) single cream, 5 eggs (5 yolks and 2 whites needed), 300ml (½pt) milk, bread to give 200g (8oz) breadcrumbs plus amount for croûtons, 50g (2oz) flour, 115g (4½oz) caster sugar or part granulated sugar, 50g (2oz) glacé cherries, 25g (1oz) candied peel, 50g (2oz) sultanas, 50g (2oz) nuts, 2tbspn salad oil, 2tbspn vinegar, 150ml (¼pt) red or port wine, 2tbspn sherry, redcurrant jelly, 675-900g (1½-2lb) potatoes, 1 red cabbage, 2 medium onions, 2 medium carrots, lettuce, parsley, fresh or dried thyme, 1 lemon, 3 oranges, 2 medium avocados.

Cheese Board

The menus have not included cheese, but in most families cheese is chosen as part of an enjoyable meal, so add your choice of cheese or cheeses plus butter and biscuits to the list of foods required. A typical French menu would offer cheese before the dessert, as opposed to Britain where it is served after the dessert. I feel there are occasions when the French tradition is good, ie when the main course is strongly flavoured, as the Jugged Hare in the menu above. On other occasions cheese makes a fitting end to the meal. For suggestions on choice of cheese, see Menu 41.

Viennoise Pudding

For the caramel
75g (3oz) granulated or caster sugar
3tbspn water

For the pudding
300ml (½pt) milk
300ml (½pt) single cream
100g (4oz) bread (weight without crusts)
50g (2oz) glacé cherries
25g (1oz) candied peel
50g (2oz) nuts
4 egg yolks
2 egg whites
40g (1½oz) caster sugar
50g (2oz) sultanas
2tbspn sherry

To Freeze Ahead

Jugged Hare, like many cooked stews, freezes perfectly; if preparing especially for freezing, add the wine after defrosting as alcohol tends to lose potency in freezing.
Forcemeat Balls: freeze on a flat dish, then pack.
Croûtons: freeze as Forcemeat Balls.
Viennoise Pudding freezes extremely well if you follow the recipe given (which includes single cream as well as milk).

A dry sherry is pleasant with the creamy fish pâté. Choose a really good red wine for the beef; a little could be added to the gravy, if it can be spared. The red wines from the Rioja area of Spain are particularly good.

Smoked Mackerel Pâté

1 large smoked mackerel
1 garlic clove
25g (1oz) butter
150ml (5fl oz) yoghurt
1tbspn horseradish cream (optional)
1tbspn lemon juice
cayenne pepper

To garnish
lettuce
lemon wedges

Variations
1 Use sieved cottage cheese instead of yoghurt; this gives a firmer pâté.
2 Kipper Pâté: use 1-2 cooked kippers instead of mackerel.

Roast Topside of Beef

2kg (4-4½lb) topside of beef*
50g (2oz) dripping or fat

*This is enough for a cold supper or lunch during the week that follows.

Yorkshire Pudding

For the batter
100g (4oz) plain flour
pinch salt
1 egg
300ml (½pt) milk

25g (1oz) dripping or fat

Variation
Use 2 eggs and deduct 2tbspn milk.

Roast Potatoes and Roast Parsnips

450-675g (1-1½lb) potatoes
75g (3oz) dripping or fat
450-675g (1-1½lb) parsnips
salt

Menu 6

Serves 4-6

Smoked Mackerel Pâté

Roast Topside of Beef with Yorkshire Pudding
Roast Potatoes – Roast Parsnips
Brussels Sprouts

Apple Pie and Cream

Smoked Mackerel Pâté

Skin the mackerel, remove the flesh and flake this finely. Peel and crush the garlic, melt the butter. Blend all the ingredients in a basin, liquidiser or food processor to give a smooth pâté. Garnish with lettuce and lemon wedges. Serve with toast and butter.

Roast Topside of Beef

As this is a lean joint of beef you are well advised to use a small amount of fat. If roasting the potatoes around the joint, you will also need to add the amount of fat given under the ingredients for roast vegetables. When roasting rib or sirloin of beef, where there is a fair distribution of lean and fat, I would avoid adding extra fat, except when roasting potatoes around the meat. The fat is certainly not necessary for rib and sirloin, particularly if roasting in a covered tin or foil or a roaster bag. Simply grease the foil or bag and roast the meat as described on page 10. Use Temperature 1, the hot oven, in this menu as the Yorkshire Pudding, roast vegetables and pie require this higher temperature. Serve with thin gravy (see page 10).

Yorkshire Pudding

Mix together the ingredients for the batter. Divide the fat between the 4 large Yorkshire Pudding tins (shown on page 2). Since this menu could so easily be stretched to serve 6 people you would need an extra 2 smaller tins and the same amount of batter. Heat the tins thoroughly in the oven, pour in the batter. You can raise the temperature slightly for 5-6 minutes at this stage – it will not spoil the rest of the food. A piece of foil could be placed over the apple pie if already in the oven. Bake the puddings for approximately 15 minutes until well risen and brown. Return the heat to the normal setting after the puddings start to rise.

Roast Potatoes

Peel and well dry the potatoes. Heat the fat in a separate tin unless roasting around the meat. Put in the potatoes and roll round in the fat so they are completely coated. Roast for ¾-1 hour, depending upon the size.

Roast Parsnips

Peel the parsnips; if large, halve lengthways. It is a good idea to par-boil this vegetable before roasting. Put into boiling salted water, cook steadily for 15 minutes. Drain and dry on absorbent paper, then roast as potatoes for 35-45 minutes. Both vegetables can be put into the same tin or around the meat, if space permits.

Brussels Sprouts

Cut the base of the sprouts; take off any discoloured or tough-looking outer leaves. If the sprouts are large it is advisable to mark the stalk at the base of each sprout with a cross; this enables them to cook more rapidly and easily. Read the comments in Menu 43 about soaking and cooking green vegetables. Use only about 2.5cm (1in) water in the pan, with a little salt; bring to the boil, add the sprouts and cook as rapidly as possible. Cover the pan during this time. Small sprouts take only about 4 minutes if you like them pleasantly firm and nutty. Drain and top with butter.

Apple Pie

Make the pastry as described in Menu 26. Peel and thinly slice the apples, put into the pie dish; add any of the flavourings suggested, then the water and sugar, stir lightly to distribute the sugar evenly. Add a pie support if necessary (see Menu 48). Cover the pie with the pastry and bake for a total of 35-40 minutes. Allow 15-20 minutes in the hot oven, reduce the heat to moderate, 180°C, 350°F, Gas Mark 4, when serving the main course. Top with a little sugar; serve with cream.

To Make Sunday Easier

1 Make the pâté one or two days beforehand if not freezing this.
2 Simmer any beef bones supplied to make stock for gravy.
3 Prepare the Apple Pie on Saturday, or, if more convenient, make and cook this to serve cold or reheat for a short time in the oven.

Foods Required

Approximately 2kg (4-4½lb) topside of beef, 1 large smoked mackerel, 125g (5oz) butter (or 50g (2oz) butter and 75g (3oz) selected fat for pastry) plus butter for toast, 150g (6oz) fat or dripping, 150-300ml (¼-½pt) whipping or double cream, 1 egg, 300ml (½pt) milk, 150ml (¼pt) yoghurt, 275g (10oz) plain flour, 75-100g (3-4oz) caster sugar, cayenne pepper, bread for toast, horseradish cream (optional), 450-675g (1-1½lb) potatoes, 450-675g (1-1½lb) parsnips, 450g (1lb) Brussels sprouts, 1 garlic clove, lettuce, 675-900g (1½-2lb) cooking apples, 2 lemons.

Roasting Vegetables in an Automatic Oven

All this menu, with the exception of the Brussels sprouts and pâté, is shown on page 2. Often people with automatic ovens are worried as to whether they can leave vegetables like potatoes in the oven for any length of time before the heat automatically switches on. This is not a problem at all if you make sure the vegetables are well coated with melted fat, to exclude the air, before leaving them in the oven.

Brussels Sprouts

450g (1lb) Brussels sprouts
salt
25g (1oz) butter

Apple Pie

For the shortcrust pastry
175g (6oz) flour
pinch salt
75g (3oz) butter or fat
water to bind

675g-900g (1½-2lb) cooking
    apples
flavourings (see below)
4tbspn water
65-90g (2½-3½oz) caster sugar

To top pie
15g (½oz) caster sugar

Flavourings for Apple Pie
5-6 cloves; strips of lemon rind or a little lemon juice; 2-3tbspn sultanas, honey or golden syrup instead of sugar.

If you come from the North of England you will probably serve cheese with the pie, for the saying is: 'An apple pie without cheese is like a kiss without a squeeze.'

To Freeze Ahead

Smoked Mackerel Pâté: freeze for up to 2-3 weeks only.
Beef: frozen beef is excellent. Defrost before cooking.
Apple Pie: either prepare and freeze or make and bake the pie, allow to cool, freeze, then wrap. Defrost before reheating.

Serve a dry sherry with the Melon Cocktail.

Choose a full-bodied red wine to accompany the Steak and Kidney Pudding. As this is a traditional British dish, why not try a British wine? There are excellent ones available.

Menu 7

Serves 6

Melon Cocktail

Steak and Kidney Pudding
Parsley Potatoes—Carrot Sticks
Haricot Verts

Dried Fruit Compôte and Cream

Melon Cocktail

For the dressing
2tbspn mayonnaise (see Menu 34)
2tbspn yoghurt or soured cream
2tspn lemon juice

1 small honeydew melon
1 small avocado
50g (2oz) peeled prawns
part of lettuce heart

To garnish
6 lemon wedges

Variation
Mix the melon with segments of grapefruit, orange and diced fresh pineapple. Omit the dressing.

Steak and Kidney Pudding

For the suet-crust pastry
225-300g (8-10oz) flour, plain or self-raising
pinch salt
100-150g (4-5oz) shredded suet (always use half the amount of suet to flour)
water to mix

For the filling
675g (1½lb) stewing steak
225g (8oz) ox kidney
1tbspn flour
salt and pepper
stock or water

Variation
Game and Steak Pudding: dice the flesh from a pheasant or large grouse, blend with 225g (8oz) stewing steak, cook as recipe.

Melon Cocktail

Mix together the mayonnaise, yoghurt or soured cream and lemon juice. Remove the seeds from the melon; scoop out, then dice the pulp, or cut this out with a vegetable scoop to make small balls. Skin and dice the avocado, put into the dressing immediately; add the prawns. Do not add the melon to the dressing until you are just filling the glasses and do not coat this—the contrasting colour is pretty. Shred the lettuce very finely, put into 6 glasses, top with the melon mixture. Garnish with lemon wedges.

Steak and Kidney Pudding

The amounts given for pastry depend upon whether you like a thin or thick crust. Self-raising flour or plain flour with 2 level tspn baking powder gives a well-puffed crust, whereas plain flour gives a more delicate one.

Sift the flour, or flour and baking powder (see above), with the salt into a mixing bowl. Add the suet and enough water to give a soft rolling consistency. Roll out and use just three-quarters to line a 1.2-1.5 litre (2-2½pt) lightly greased basin.

Dice the meats, blend with the flour and a little salt and pepper. Put into the pastry-lined basin. Add enough stock or water to come about two-thirds up the basin. Roll out the remaining dough into a round sufficiently large to cover the filling. Moisten the edges of the pastry with water, press the pastry round in position. Cover with greased greaseproof paper and foil. Steam over boiling water for 4½-5 hours. If you like extra gravy with the pudding, see the comments on page 10.

Parsley Potatoes

Peel or scrape the potatoes or cook in their skins. Put into boiling salted water, cover the saucepan. Cook steadily for about 25 minutes, or until just tender. Remember the old adage 'A potato boiled is a potato spoiled', so never allow the water to boil rapidly during cooking. A sprig of mint may be added to new potatoes.

Strain the potatoes carefully. Melt the butter in a saucepan, add the parsley. Either spoon over the potatoes in the vegetable dish, or return the potatoes to the saucepan and turn gently in the parsley mixture, then serve.

Creamed Potatoes

Cook the old potatoes as above; strain. Return to the saucepan and heat very gently for 1-2 minutes so they dry out. Mash with a fork or a potato masher until smooth and free from lumps, or sieve. Heat the milk with the butter or margarine in a second saucepan. Gradually beat into the mashed potatoes with a wooden spoon; season well. The heated milk and strong beating action produce a beautifully light and white mixture.

Carrot Sticks and Haricot Verts

Peel the carrots, cut into long strips, as shown on page 87. Cook steadily in boiling salted water for 20 minutes; top with butter. The tender green beans, often known as 'green beans', need just topping and tailing if fresh, but no preparation if frozen. Cook steadily in boiling salted water for 10 minutes if fresh, or as directed if frozen. Top with butter.

Dried Fruit Compôte

By traditional method Cover the fruit with the 1.2 litre (2pt) cold water, leave soaking overnight, then put into a saucepan; check there is plenty of liquid. Add the sugar, cover the saucepan and simmer gently for 1½ hours. The fruit can be cooked in a covered casserole in a slow oven, 150°C, 300°C, Gas Mark 2, for the same time.

Using a microwave cooker There is no need to soak the fruit; simply put into a ceramic dish or bowl and add the 450-600ml (¾-1pt) water (the amount depends upon how much juice is required). Cover with clingfilm. Cook on HIGH for 5 minutes, add the sugar, cover again and continue cooking for 7 minutes. Allow to stand for 30 minutes. Serve hot or cold with cream.

To Make Sunday Easier

1 Make the Steak and Kidney Pudding; put into the refrigerator and cook on Sunday. If more convenient, cook for at least 2½ hours (see To Freeze Ahead), then continue cooking on Sunday. Make stock if you like additional gravy.
2 Put dried fruit to soak, ready to cook on Sunday, or soak on Friday and cook on Saturday if having cold. If using a microwave cooker, cook the fruit on Saturday.

Foods Required

675g (1½lb) stewing steak, 225g (8oz) ox kidney, 50g (2oz) peeled prawns, 75-100g (3-4oz) butter, 100-150g (4-5oz) shredded suet, 150-300ml (¼-½pt) whipping or double cream, 2tbspn yoghurt or soured cream, 225-300g (8-10oz) flour (plain or self-raising), 50g (2oz) caster sugar, 2tbspn mayonnaise (see Menu 34), 450-675g (1-1½lb) old or new potatoes, 450-675g (1-1½lb) carrots, 450g (1lb) haricot verts, lettuce heart, parsley, 1 small honeydew melon, 1 avocado, 2 lemons, 450g (1lb) mixed dried fruit.

Parsley Potatoes

450-675g (1-1½lb) old or new potatoes
salt
25-50g (1-2oz) butter
1-2tbspn chopped parsley

Variations

Creamed Potatoes
450-675g (1-1½lb) old potatoes
salt and pepper
3-5tbspn milk
25-50g (1-2oz) butter or margarine

Creamed Parsley Potatoes
Add 2tbspn chopped parsley to the creamed potatoes.

Carrot Sticks and Haricot Verts

450-675g (1-1½lb) carrots
450g (1lb) fresh or frozen haricot verts
salt
50g (2oz) butter

Dried Fruit Compôte

450g (1lb) mixed dried fruit
1.2 litre (2pt) water or 450-600ml (¾-1pt) water (see method)
50g (2oz) caster sugar

To Freeze Ahead

Steak and Kidney Pudding: make when convenient; do not cook, freeze. It is better to defrost before cooking.

If preferred, steam the pudding for at least 2½ hours; this makes sure the pastry is well cooked. Cool, then freeze. Defrost and complete the cooking.

Aubergines Casalinga
2 medium aubergines
2 medium onions
2-3 garlic cloves
4 large tomatoes
1tbspn oil
50g (2oz) butter
3tbspn white wine
1tspn tomato purée
1tbspn chopped parsley
½tspn chopped basil
salt and pepper
4tbspn grated Parmesan cheese

Veal Chops with Rosemary
2tbspn flour
2tspn chopped rosemary
salt and pepper
4 thick veal chops
1tbspn oil
75g (3oz) butter
150ml (¼pt) chicken stock
150ml (¼pt) soured cream
1-2tspn French mustard
4 sprigs rosemary

Vegetable Risotto
225g (8oz) long grain rice
600ml (1pt) chicken stock
salt and pepper
3 medium carrots
100g (4oz) frozen peas

Caramelled Oranges
8 large oranges (preferably seedless)
300ml (½pt) water
75g (3oz) granulated or caster sugar
8 Maraschino or glacé cherries

To Freeze Ahead
Aubergines Casalinga can be frozen in oven-proof dishes. Rice or dishes based on rice can be frozen for up to 3 months. Cook, cool and pack. Freeze lightly, then separate the grains with a fork.

Menu 8	Aubergines Casalinga
Serves 4	Veal Chops with Rosemary Vegetables Risotto – Green Salad
	Caramelled Oranges

Aubergines Casalinga
Thinly slice the aubergines, then halve each slice (to avoid any bitter taste of aubergines see Menu 1). Peel and chop the onions and garlic. Skin and slice the tomatoes. Heat the oil and butter in a large frying pan. Fry the aubergines, onions and garlic until nearly tender. Add the rest of the ingredients, except the cheese. Cook until tomatoes are soft. Spoon into 4 dishes, add the cheese. Serve with toast.

Veal Chops with Rosemary
Blend the flour, rosemary, salt and pepper and press into both sides of the chops. Heat the oil and butter in a large frying pan; fry the chops for 12-15 minutes until golden in colour and almost tender. Blend the stock, cream and mustard; pour into the pan, lower the heat and stir until the sauce thickens slightly. Serve the chops with the sauce and top with rosemary sprigs.

Vegetable Risotto
Put the rice, cold stock, salt and pepper into a good-sized saucepan. Bring to the boil, stir briskly. Cover the pan, simmer for 10 minutes. Peel and grate the carrots, add to the rice with the peas. Simmer for a further 10-15 minutes.

For Green Salad, see Menu 37.

Caramelled Oranges
Cut the peel from the oranges; discard any pith, then slice the rind from 2-3 oranges into matchsticks. Simmer in the water until soft and the liquid reduced to half. Make a light caramel as described in Menu 5, add the peel and liquid, heat for 2-3 minutes. Meanwhile, slice the oranges; put together and secure with cocktail sticks. Top with the cherries, peel and liquid. Serve cold with cream.

To Make Sunday Easier
1 Prepare Aubergines Casalinga and cover, unless freezing the dish.
2 Prepare caramel only; do not make the sweet a day beforehand.

Foods Required
4 thick veal chops, 125g (5oz) butter, 4tbspn grated Parmesan cheese, 150ml (¼pt) soured cream plus cream to serve with dessert, 2tbspn flour, 75g (3oz) granulated or caster sugar, 225g (8oz) long grain rice, 1tspn tomato purée, 2tbspn oil, French mustard, 8 Maraschino or glacé cherries, 3 tbspn white wine, 2 medium aubergines, 2 medium onions, 2-3 garlic cloves, 3 medium carrots, 100g (4oz) frozen peas, 4 large tomatoes, ingredients for Green Salad (see Menu 37), parsley, basil, rosemary, 8 large oranges (preferably seedless).

Menu 8
Aubergines Casalinga; Veal Chops with Rosemary, Vegetable Risotto; Caramelled Oranges

Serve a sparkling white wine
with this rather special buffet
meal. There are good wines from
the Loire district, German hocks
and Freixenet from Spain.

Seafood Cocktail

For the Mary Rose Dressing
4tbspn double cream
8tbspn mayonnaise (see Menu
   34)
1tbspn lemon juice
1tbspn dry sherry
few drops Tabasco sauce
4tbspn fresh or 2tbspn concentrated tomato purée
   or ketchup
salt and pepper

175g (6oz) fresh salmon
175g (6oz) peeled prawns
100g (4oz) crabmeat
lettuce

To garnish
8 lemon slices

Bortsch

450g (1lb) raw beetroot
4 medium onions
4 medium carrots
3 sticks celery
450g (1lb) tomatoes
75g (3oz) butter
2.4 litres (4pt) beef stock
3 bay leaves
2tbspn lemon juice or white
   wine vinegar
salt and pepper
2-3tspn sugar

To garnish
300ml (10fl oz) yoghurt
1 medium cooked beetroot
4tbspn chopped parsley

Turkey Tetrazzini

225g (8oz) macaroni
salt and pepper
150g (5oz) turkey fat or butter
75g (3oz) flour
1.2 litres (2pt) milk
150ml (¼pt) double cream
225g (8oz) button mushrooms
900g (2lb) cooked turkey
50g (2oz) blanched almonds
6tbspn white wine
75g (3oz) Cheddar cheese

Menu 9

Serves 8

Seafood Cocktail

Bortsch

Turkey Tetrazzini—Julienne Salad

Fruit Galette—Sherry Trifle

Seafood Cocktail

Blend together the ingredients for the dressing. Flake the salmon. Mix the dressing with the salmon, prawns and crabmeat, allow to stand for 1 hour. Shred the lettuce very finely, then chop into small pieces; remember, this cocktail is eaten with a small spoon and it is extremely difficult to cope with long strips of lettuce. Put the lettuce into 8 glasses or a large bowl; top with the fish mixture and garnish with the lemon.

Bortsch

Peel and coarsely grate the beetroot, onions and carrots; neatly dice the celery; skin and dice the tomatoes. Heat the butter, fry the vegetables for several minutes; do not allow to discolour. Add the stock, bay leaves, lemon juice or vinegar, salt, pepper and sugar. Cover the saucepan and simmer gently for 45 minutes. Remove the bay leaves and serve. Top with the yoghurt. Peel and grate the cooked beetroot; spoon over the yoghurt, add the parsley.

Turkey Tetrazzini

Cook the macaroni in boiling salted water. Heat 75g (3oz) of the turkey fat or butter, stir in the flour, cook over a low heat for 2-3 minutes, then gradually blend in the milk. Stir as the sauce comes to the boil, add the cream, salt and pepper to taste. Meanwhile, heat the remaining fat or butter and cook the mushrooms; add to the sauce. Dice the turkey neatly, stir into the sauce together with the macaroni, almonds and wine. Spoon into a 2.4-3 litre (4-5pt) oven-proof serving dish. Top with the cheese. Heat for about 45 minutes in the centre of a very moderate oven, 160°C, 325°F, Gas Mark 3; keep hot in a slow oven.

Julienne Salad Follow directions for Mixed Salad in Menu 14, but cut ingredients into matchstick pieces easily eaten with a fork.

Fruit Galette

Sift the flour and salt into a basin, add the lemon juice and water to make an elastic rolling consistency. Roll out to a neat oblong, place the butter in the centre part of the dough. Bring up the bottom third, bring down the top third, so enclosing the butter. Turn the pastry at right angles, seal the ends, then 'rib' the dough (depress at regular intervals with the rolling pin). Roll out again to the oblong shape. Repeat the folding action, seal the ends and 'rib' again. Puff pastry should have a total of 7 foldings and 7 rollings. You will need to cover the dough and put it into the refrigerator to chill between these stages.

To make 2 galettes divide the pastry in half; roll out each half until just under 0.5cm (¼in) in thickness. Cut into large rounds (you can obtain this by placing a large plate on each piece of pastry and cutting round it). Place each piece of pastry on an ungreased baking tray. Score the top lightly with a knife; this encourages the pastry to rise evenly. Cover with clingfilm or foil, chill in the refrigerator for a short time. Whisk the egg whites until frothy and brush over the pastry; sprinkle with the sugar. Bake just above the centre of a hot to very hot oven, 220-230°C, 425-450°F, Gas Mark 7-8, until the pastry begins to rise. Lower the heat to moderate, 180°C, 350°F, Gas Mark 4, and cook for a further 10 minutes, or until the pastry is crisp. Remove from the tray to cool; repeat with the second round.

Prepare the fruits. Put the jelly, water and lemon juice into a saucepan, stir over a low heat until dissolved; cool, but do not allow to stiffen. Brush about one-third of the glaze over the pastry, put the fruit in position; brush with the remaining glaze. Whip the cream, serve with the dessert.

Sherry Trifle

Split the sponge cakes, sandwich together with the jam, put into 8 individual dishes. Moisten with the sherry. Flake the nuts and add half to the sponges together with the ratafia biscuits. Make a custard with the whole eggs, egg yolks, sugar, milk and vanilla flavouring in the top of a double saucepan (see Menu 46). Pour the warm custard over the sponges, allow to cool. Whip the cream, spread half over the custard; pipe the remainder on top and decorate with the remaining nuts, glacé cherries and angelica.

To Make Sunday Easier

1 Prepare the Mary Rose Dressing, put in a container. Cook the salmon.
2 Make the soup and cook lightly.
3 Prepare the Turkey Tetrazzini; put into the cooking dish, cover. Any dish containing pasta should have a little extra liquid (about 6tbspn in this case) if prepared ahead; reheat.
4 Take time to make the pastry; bake galettes ahead. Do not top with fruit until Sunday.

Foods Required

Turkey to give 900g (2lb) when cooked, salmon to give 175g (6oz) when cooked, 175g (6oz) peeled prawns, 100g (4oz) crabmeat, 450g (1lb) butter or 300g (11oz) if using turkey fat, 75g (3oz) Cheddar cheese, 750ml (1¼pt) double cream plus 4tbspn, 4 eggs, 2 litres (3½pt) milk, 300ml (½pt) yoghurt, 300g (11oz) plain flour, 75g (3oz) sugar plus 4tbspn, 225g (8oz) macaroni, 8 trifle sponge cakes, 4tbspn jam, 225g (8oz) redcurrant jelly, 100g (4oz) blanched almonds, few glacé cherries, small piece angelica, 25g (1oz) ratafia biscuits, vanilla pod or essence, 6tbspn white wine, 1tbspn dry sherry, 6tbspn sweet sherry, white wine vinegar if not using lemon juice, 8tbspn mayonnaise (see Menu 34), 3 bay leaves, Tabasco sauce, 4tbspn fresh or 2tbspn concentrated tomato purée or ketchup, lettuce, 450g (1lb) raw and 1 medium cooked beetroot, 4 medium onions, 4 medium carrots, 3 sticks celery, 450g (1lb) tomatoes, 225g (8oz) button mushrooms, ingredients for Julienne (Mixed) Salad (see Menu 14), parsley, 4 lemons, 1.1-1.3kg (2½-3lb) seasonal dessert fruit.

Fruit Galette

For the puff pastry
225g (8oz) plain flour
pinch salt
1tbspn lemon juice
water to mix
225g (8oz) unsalted butter
2 egg whites
3tbspn caster sugar

1.1-1.3kg (2½-3lb) seasonal ripe fresh dessert fruit (grapes, imported peaches, etc)
225g (8oz) redcurrant jelly
150ml (¼pt) water
2tbspn lemon juice
300ml (½pt) double cream

Sherry Trifle

8 trifle sponge cakes
3-4tbspn jam
6tbspn sweet sherry
25-50g (1-2oz) blanched almonds
25g (1oz) ratafia biscuits

For the custard
2 whole eggs
2 egg yolks
75g (3oz) sugar
900ml (1½pt) milk
vanilla pod or vanilla essence

300ml (½pt) double cream
few glacé cherries
angelica
blanched almonds (see method)

To Freeze Ahead

Bortsch freezes well.
Turkey Tetrazzini freezes very well; defrost before reheating.
Galettes: freeze uncooked or cooked pastry without toppings.

A red Burgundy, such as Mâcon or a Rhône Hermitage or Spanish red wine would blend well with the lamb.

Prawn Scallops
pastry made with 100g (4oz) flour, etc (see Menu 26)
100g (4oz) peeled prawns
3tbspn thick mayonnaise (see Menu 34)
1tbspn chopped parsley
1tbspn dry sherry
2tbspn cream cheese

To garnish
lettuce
lemon slices

Dijon Lamb
loin of lamb
1tbspn Dijon mustard
2tbspn apple jelly
1tspn chopped mint
fat for roasting onions and potatoes

Cauliflower Polonaise
2 eggs
1 cauliflower
salt
25g (1oz) butter
25g (1oz) soft breadcrumbs
1-2tbspn chopped parsley

Rhubarb and Ginger Fool
150ml (¼pt) double cream
300ml (½pt) thick sweetened custard sauce
450ml (¾pt) thick sweetened rhubarb purée
50g (2oz) crystallised ginger

To Freeze Ahead
Baked pastry shells.

Menu 10

Serves 4

Prawn Scallops

Dijon Lamb
Roast Potatoes and Onions
Cauliflower Polonaise

Rhubarb and Ginger Fool

Prawn Scallops
Roll out the pastry and line 4 scallop shells. Bake 'blind' until crisp and golden (see Menu 26). Allow to cool. Defrost and drain prawns if frozen. Blend the prawns with the other ingredients (omit sherry for children's portions). Spoon into the pastry case just before lunch. Serve cold or put into the oven for 10-15 minutes. Garnish with lettuce and lemon slices.

Dijon Lamb
Roast the lamb as the timing for Temperature 1 on page 10. Take out of the oven 15 minutes before the end of the cooking period. Blend together the mustard, jelly and mint. Spread over the lamb, return to the oven to complete the cooking.

   Cook roast onions and potatoes as described for Roast Potatoes in Menu 6.

Cauliflower Polonaise
Hard-boiled, shell and chop the eggs. Cook the cauliflower in boiling salted water, then strain and put into the serving dish. Meanwhile, heat the butter in a saucepan, add the breadcrumbs, fry until golden. Blend with the eggs and parsley. Spoon over the cauliflower.

Rhubarb and Ginger Fool
Whip the cream. Make the custard sauce; allow to cool. Blend the custard and smooth rhubarb purée together; add half the cream. Chop the ginger; add most of this to the rhubarb mixture. (This could be omitted for children's portions.) Spoon into sundae glasses. Decorate with the remaining cream and chopped ginger.

To Make Sunday Easier
1   Bake pastry scallop shells earlier in the week.
2   Prepare ingredients for topping cauliflower on Saturday.
3   Make Rhubarb and Ginger Fool; it is nicer well chilled.

Foods Required
Loin of lamb (8-10 chops), 100g (4oz) peeled prawns, 25g (1oz) butter, 50g (2oz) fat, ingredients for pastry (see Menu 26), 50g (2oz) cream cheese, 150ml (¼pt) double cream, 300ml (½pt) milk, 2 eggs, 100g (4oz) sugar, bread to give 25g (1oz) crumbs, 2tbspn apple jelly, Dijon mustard, mayonnaise (see Menu 34), custard powder, 50g (2oz) crystallised ginger, dry sherry, 450g (1lb) onions, lettuce, 675g (1½lb) potatoes, 1 cauliflower, parsley, mint (or bottled mint), 1 lemon, 450-675g (1-1½lb) rhubarb.

Menu 10
Prawn Scallops; Dijon Lamb, Roast Onions and Potatoes, Cauliflower Polonaise; Rhubarb and Ginger Fool

Mulligatawny Soup

1 large onion
1 small dessert apple
1 small carrot
50g (2oz) fat, preferably lamb
  fat
40g (1½oz) flour
1tbspn curry powder
900ml (1½pt) lamb stock
salt and pepper
1tbspn chutney
25g (1oz) sultanas
little lemon juice or vinegar
pinch sugar

To garnish
fried croûtons or 1-2tbspn
  cooked rice

Variations
1 Use other fat if lamb fat not
available.
2 Use chicken stock if lamb
stock not available.

Mixed Grill

Have 3-4 different ingredients
  for each person; select from
  lamb, pork or veal chops or
  cutlets, fingers of tender
  steak, small slices of calves'
  or lambs' liver, lambs'
  kidneys, sausages, bacon
  rashers
50-75g (2-3oz) butter or
  margarine
salt and pepper
allow 1-2 tomatoes and about
  4 mushrooms per person

To garnish
watercress

Sauté Potatoes

450-550g (1-1¼lb) potatoes
salt

For frying
50-75g (2-3oz) fat

To garnish
chopped parsley

Menu 11	Mulligatawny Soup
Serves 4-5	Mixed Grill with Sauté Potatoes Tomatoes – Mushrooms – Creamed Spinach
	Fruit Syrup Pudding with Orange Sauce

Mulligatawny Soup

Peel and chop the onion and apple; peel and dice the carrot. Heat the fat in a large saucepan, fry the vegetables and apple for several minutes, then blend in the flour and curry powder. Stir over a low heat for 2-3 minutes, then gradually add the stock and the rest of the ingredients. Bring to the boil, stir once or twice and simmer for approximately 45 minutes. Sieve or put the ingredients into a liquidiser or food processor until a smooth purée. Taste and adjust the amount of seasoning, lemon juice or vinegar and sweet flavours. Top with crisp croûtons or rice.

Mixed Grill

Look at the various meats to be cooked and decide the order in which they should be grilled. If possible, try to have all the foods ready at the same time. Melt enough butter or margarine to brush over the lean food, add a little salt and pepper. Pre-heat the grill; brush the grid with a little butter so the foods do not stick to this. Either halve the tomatoes, or leave whole depending upon the size; prepare the mushrooms (see comments about preparing and grilling mushrooms in Menu 12). Either put these foods around the meats on the grid of the grill pan or cook in the grill pan itself under the grid. In the latter case cook the mushrooms and tomatoes for a few minutes before placing the grid with the first meats on top; this makes certain that the mushrooms and tomatoes will be adequately cooked with the meats. If you have a large grill pan you will be able to start the cooking with the chops, then add the other foods in order of cooking time. If you have a smaller grill, cook the chops, sausages and kidneys first and keep hot while cooking the steak, liver and bacon which can spoil by being kept waiting. Always brush lean meats with butter or fat at least once during cooking as well as before placing under the grill. Garnish with watercress.

Sauté Potatoes

Peel or scrape the potatoes; cook steadily in boiling salted water until only just cooked – they must be sufficiently firm to cut into neat slices that do not break. Strain and cool sufficiently to handle or leave until cold. Cut into 0.5-1cm (¼-½in) thick slices. Heat the fat in a large frying pan and fry the potatoes until hot, crisp and golden on both sides. Top with chopped parsley. It is not usual to drain sauté potatoes, like other fried foods, on absorbent paper.

Creamed Spinach

Wash the spinach well in cold water. Cook in the water adhering to the leaves. Add a little salt only. Strain and chop very finely. Heat the butter in the saucepan, stir in the flour and cook for 2-3 minutes, then gradually stir in the milk or cream. Continue stirring over a low heat until a thick sauce. Add the spinach, blend thoroughly, heat and season well.

Fruit Syrup Pudding with Orange Sauce

Grate the top 'zest' from the oranges. Halve the fruit and squeeze out the juice. Use 4tbspn for the pudding. Any juice left over may be used in the sauce. Cream together the butter or margarine, sugar and orange rind until soft and light. Gradually beat in the eggs; sift the flour, or flour and baking powder. Fold into the creamed mixture together with the 4tbspn orange juice and the dried fruit. Grease a 1 litre (1¾pt) basin, spoon the 3tbspn syrup into the bottom of the basin; add the pudding mixture; cover and steam for 1½-1¾ hours. Turn out and serve with the sauce. To make the sauce simply heat the fruit juices and syrup together.

To make Sunday Easier

1 Make the soup and cook croûtons unless both soup and croûtons are being frozen.
2 Cook potatoes ready to slice and sauté; keep in the refrigerator.
3 The pudding can be mixed, covered and kept in the refrigerator; the sauce can be made.

Foods Required

Meats for Mixed Grill (see recipe), 200-225g (7½-8½oz) butter or margarine plus extra butter if cooking croûtons in butter, oil or fat if not frying croûtons in butter, 50-75g (2-3oz) fat plus fat for soup if lamb fat not available, 2 large eggs, 150ml (¼pt) milk or single cream, 240g (8½oz) flour plus baking powder if using plain flour, 110g (4oz) caster sugar plus pinch, bread for croûtons if not garnishing soup with rice, curry powder, 75g (3oz) sultanas, 50g (2oz) seedless raisins, 9tbspn golden syrup (approximately 275g (9oz)), chutney, little rice if not garnishing soup with croûtons, vinegar if not using lemon juice in soup, 1 large onion, 1 small carrot, 450-550g (1-1¼lb) potatoes, 675g (1½lb) spinach, 8-10 tomatoes, approximately 225g (8oz) mushrooms, watercress, parsley, 1 small dessert apple, 2-3 large oranges (8tbspn juice needed), 1 lemon to give 1tbspn juice plus squeeze if not using vinegar in soup.

Using a Microwave Cooker for Puddings

A microwave cooker can be used very successfully to make many steamed puddings similar to the recipe in this menu. The cooking time for this particular recipe would be approximately 7 minutes on HIGH or until the pudding is well risen.

Creamed Spinach

675g (1½lb) spinach
salt and pepper
40g (1½oz) butter
25g (1oz) flour
150ml (¼pt) milk or single cream

Fruit Syrup Pudding

2 large oranges
110g (4oz) butter or margarine
110g (4oz) caster sugar
2 large eggs
175g (6oz) self-raising flour or plain flour with 1½tspn baking powder
50g (2oz) seedless raisins
50g (2oz) sultanas
3tbspn golden syrup

For the sauce
4tbspn orange juice
1tbspn lemon juice
6tbspn golden syrup

To Freeze Ahead

Mulligatawny Soup: make and freeze when you have lamb stock available. Garnish of croûtons or rice: freeze separately; add when reheating. Mixed Grill cannot be pre-cooked and frozen, but it is an excellent dish in which to use frozen meats.
Fruit Syrup Pudding: either freeze uncooked or cooked mixture and the sauce.

Cooking Steamed Puddings

Always grease the basin or container well before adding the mixture. Allow plenty of space for the pudding mixture to rise in the basin. Cover carefully with greased grease-proof paper and/or foil.

When cooking a pudding, as in this menu, make certain the water boils rapidly for the first third to half of the cooking period; after this time the water can boil steadily. Keep the saucepan under the steamer filled with boiling water.

Brunch, a combination of breakfast and lunch, is an adaptable meal so offer tea, coffee or fruit juice. Some people may enjoy chilled beer, cider or white wine.

Hawaiian Grapefruit
2 large grapefruit
3 rings canned pineapple
little brown sugar

Brunch Grill
4-8 tomatoes
100g (4oz) mushrooms
4-8 rashers streaky or back
  bacon
4-8 sausages
salt and pepper
little butter or fat (see method)
4-8 eggs

Variation
Fry, rather than grill, the foods. Table cookers enable you to do this at the table, or use a microwave cooker.

Potato Cakes
450g (1lb) old potatoes
salt and pepper
2tbspn milk
25g (1oz) butter or margarine
1 egg yolk
approximately 25g (1oz) flour

For frying
50g (2oz) fat

Variation
Add chopped herbs to flavour.

To Freeze Ahead
Potato Cakes: open-freeze, then pack.
Rolls: keep a supply in the freezer.

Using a Microwave Cooker
Use your microwave cooker to:

a) Heat the grapefruit and rolls.
b) Cook the bacon and tomatoes.

+--+
| # Menu 12   Hawaiian Grapefruit |
| |
| *Serves 4*   Brunch Grill – Potato Cakes |
| |
| Rolls – Butter – Cheese – Fruit |
+--+

Hawaiian Grapefruit
Halve the grapefruit, spoon out the segments of fruit. Dice the pineapple, mix with the grapefruit. Spoon back into the grapefruit skins; sprinkle with brown sugar and put under the grill for a few minutes.

Brunch Grill
Halve the tomatoes; wipe the mushrooms and trim the ends of the stalks. As there is an appreciable amount of flavour in the skins, good quality mushrooms should not be skinned. Derind the bacon. Modern sausages do not need pricking (unless specifically stated on the packet). You can put the mushrooms and tomatoes into the pan under the grill pan grid on which the bacon and sausages are cooked. Season lightly, top with a very little butter or fat and start cooking under the grill for 2-3 minutes. Put the sausages on the grid and cook until beginning to brown, then add the bacon rashers and complete the cooking.

Do not cook the eggs until the Potato Cakes and the rest of the ingredients are almost, if not entirely, cooked. Heat a little butter or fat in the frying pan. Break each egg into a cup or saucer and carefully tip into the pan. Tilt the pan slightly as each egg goes into the fat so the white sets in a good shape.

Potato Cakes
Peel the potatoes; cook steadily in boiling salted water until just soft; strain and return to the pan. Heat gently for 1-2 minutes to make sure the potatoes are dry and floury, then mash. Heat the milk and butter or margarine and beat into the potatoes. You can add an egg yolk to give a softer texture. Season well and divide into 8 portions. When cool, form into round cakes with well-floured hands. Heat the fat in the frying pan and fry the cakes until very hot and crisp and brown on either side.

To Make Sunday Easier
1   Prepare grapefruit ahead; add the sugar just before cooking.
2   Make and chill Potato Cakes if not being frozen.

Foods Required
4-8 sausages, 4-8 rashers streaky or back bacon, butter for serving with rolls plus extra for grilling food if not using fat, 50g (2oz) fat plus extra for grilling food if not using butter, cheese (see Menu 41), 5-9 eggs (4-8 whole eggs, plus 1 yolk), 2tbspn milk, 25g (1oz) flour, little brown sugar, 3 rings canned pineapple, rolls as required, 4-8 tomatoes, 100g (4oz) mushrooms, 450g (1lb) old potatoes, 2 large grapefruit, fresh fruit.

Menu 11
Fruit Syrup Pudding with Orange Sauce

30

This vegetarian menu can be varied for non-vegetarians as the suggestions under the recipes. This may determine the choice of drinks. Have dry cider, fresh fruit juice, white or rosé wine for the vegetarian menu.

Savoury Choux

For the choux pastry
150ml (¼pt) water
salt and pepper
25g (1oz) margarine
75g (3oz) plain flour
2 large eggs

Fillings
See method

Stuffed Aubergines

6 medium aubergines
½tbspn olive or corn oil
salt and pepper

For the stuffing
6 eggs
2 medium onions
2 garlic cloves
3 large tomatoes
50g (2oz) margarine or
    vegetarian fat
50-75g (2-3oz) Cheddar cheese
75g (3oz) soft breadcrumbs

For the topping
50g (2oz) Cheddar cheese
40g (1½oz) crisp breadcrumbs

Variation
Add a little chopped cooked ham or salami to the filling for non-vegetarians.

Baked Tomatoes

6 medium tomatoes

Sweet Sour Carrots

450g (1lb) carrots
1 medium onion
salt and pepper
pinch of curry powder
pinch of ground cinnamon
40g (1½oz) margarine
50g (2oz) seedless raisins
1tbspn lemon juice
1tspn brown sugar

Menu 13   Savoury Choux

Serves 6

Stuffed Aubergines – Baked Tomatoes
Sweet Sour Carrots – Purée of Swedes
    Armardine

Lemon and Apricot Cheesecake

Savoury Choux

Put the water, salt, pepper and margarine into a saucepan. Heat until the margarine melts. Remove from the heat, add the flour. Return the pan to a low heat and stir until the mixture forms a smooth dry ball which leaves the sides of the pan clean. Remove the pan once more from the heat and gradually beat in the eggs. Spoon 12 rounds of mixture on to a greased and floured baking tray; if preferred, you can use a 1cm (½in) plain pipe in a large piping bag. Bake for approximately 20 minutes just above the centre of a moderate to moderately hot oven, 190-200°C, 375-400°F, Gas Mark 5-6, until well risen and firm. Slit, and if there is any slightly uncooked mixture in the buns remove this and return the buns to the oven briefly to dry out. Allow to cool.

The fillings can be varied. Vegetarians will enjoy thick vegetable purées, such as spinach, beans, peas or cottage cheese with chopped herbs and nuts. Non-vegetarians can enjoy seasoned crabmeat or prawns or diced ham blended with mayonnaise.

Stuffed Aubergines

Before halving the aubergines read the advice in Menu 1 to avoid the slightly bitter taste from the vegetable. Rinse the aubergines in cold water, dry and halve lengthways. Score the top surface lightly. Brush with a little oil, sprinkle with salt and pepper. Put into an oiled dish and bake in the centre of a moderately hot oven, 200°C, 400°F, Gas Mark 6, for about 20 minutes, or until the aubergines' centres are fairly soft. Scoop out these centres, chop finely, leaving a narrow band around the inside of the skins. Meanwhile, hard-boil, shell and chop the eggs. Peel and finely chop the onions and garlic; skin and chop the tomatoes. Heat the margarine or fat and fry the onions and garlic until very soft; do not allow to brown. Grate the cheese; mix with the fried vegetables, aubergine centres, breadcrumbs, salt and pepper. Spoon into the 12 aubergine cases. Grate the cheese for the topping; mix with the crisp breadcrumbs. Press over the filling; return to the centre of the oven and heat for a further 15-20 minutes.

Baked Tomatoes

Cook 6 medium tomatoes for 10-15 minutes.

Sweet Sour Carrots

Peel and thinly slice the carrots; peel and finely dice the onion. Put the vegetables into boiling salted water, add the spices; cook until nearly soft. Strain through a fine sieve and allow to dry. Heat the margarine, add the carrots, onion, raisins, lemon juice and sugar. Turn in the fat for several minutes or until all the ingredients are very hot, then serve.

Purée of Swedes Armardine

Peel and dice the swedes. Cook steadily in boiling salted water until tender. Drain, then return to the pan and mash. Beat in the margarine, salt and pepper to taste. Spoon into a heated serving dish. Spike with the almonds and sprinkle with the herbs.

Lemon and Apricot Cheesecake

Prepare the crumb mixture first and allow to cool. Melt the margarine, crush the biscuit crumbs. Blend together the crumbs, butter and the 25g (1oz) sugar. Put on one side. Chill a 20cm (8in) cake tin with a loose base, press the crumb mixture on to the bottom of the tin; put into the refrigerator while making the cheesecake.

Sieve the cottage cheese and blend with the cream cheese. Drain the apricots; measure out 2tbspn of the syrup. Put this into a basin with the lemon rind and juice. Sprinkle the gelatine on to the liquid; stand the basin over a pan of very hot water and allow the gelatine to dissolve. Stir well to blend. Separate the eggs; whisk the yolks with 25g (1oz) of the sugar until thick and creamy. Gradually whisk the warm gelatine mixture into the whisked yolks. Allow to cool (watch it does not set), then blend with the cheeses. Put about 8 apricot halves on one side for decoration. Dry the remaining fruit on absorbent paper, cut into thin slices, then blend with the cheesecake mixture. Whip the cream until it holds its shape. In a separate bowl whisk the egg whites until stiff; fold in the remaining 50g (2oz) sugar. Blend the cream and then the egg whites into the cheese mixture. Spoon into the cake tin; smooth flat on top. Allow to set, then carefully turn out of the tin and decorate. Halve and deseed the grapes; do not skin. Cut each apricot half into two portions. Arrange the fruit around the edge of the cheesecake.

You can pipe a border of cream on the dessert, but this is not necessary for it is sufficiently rich.

To Make Sunday Easier

1   Bake the small Savoury Choux on Saturday unless freezing; crisp for a few minutes in the oven on Sunday, then cool and fill.
2   Prepare aubergines if not freezing; cover and put in refrigerator.
3   Make the cheesecake one or two days ahead if not freezing.

Foods Required

175g (6½oz) margarine (chosen as preferred by vegetarians), 50g (2oz) butter, ½tbspn corn or olive oil, 100-150g (4-5oz) Cheddar cheese, 225g (8oz) cottage cheese, 225g (8oz) cream cheese, 150ml (¼pt) double cream plus extra to decorate cheesecake, 10 eggs, 75g (3oz) flour, 100g (4oz) caster sugar plus tspn brown sugar, bread to give 75g (3oz) soft breadcrumbs plus 40g (1½oz) crisp breadcrumbs, 100g (4oz) digestive biscuits (recipe gives crumbs as it is a good way to use up broken biscuits), 15g (½oz) gelatine, curry powder, ground cinnamon, 50g (2oz) seedless raisins, 25-50g (1-2oz) blanched almonds, 397g (14oz) can apricots, 6 medium aubergines, 2 onions, 2 garlic cloves, 450g (1lb) carrots, 450-675g (1-1½lb) swedes, 3 large tomatoes, 6 medium tomatoes, parsley, chives, 1 lemon (to give 3tbspn juice), black grapes, ingredients for filling choux (see method).

Purée of Swedes Armardine

450-675g (1-1½lb) swedes
salt and pepper
50g (2oz) margarine

To garnish
25-50g (1-2oz) blanched
   almonds
1tbspn chopped parsley
1tbspn chopped chives

Lemon and Apricot Cheesecake

For the crumb base
50g (2oz) margarine
100g (4oz) digestive crumbs
25g (1oz) sugar

For the topping
225g (8oz) cottage cheese
225g (8oz) cream cheese
397g (14oz) can apricots
1tspn finely grated lemon rind
2tbspn lemon juice
15g (½oz) gelatine
2 large eggs
75g (3oz) caster sugar
150ml (¼pt) double cream

To decorate
black grapes
apricots
whipped cream (optional)

To Freeze Ahead

Choux pastry: either before or after baking, plus fillings. Aubergines: when cooked. Cheesecake: allow to set before freezing. To remove the cheesecake from the tin push the loose base upwards with your hand or a jam jar; the outer ring of the cake tin will fall downwards and can be removed. Slide palette knife under biscuit crust to remove base of tin; easy to do when frozen.

A very dry cider would be pleasant with this meal or choose a rosé wine or very cold beer.

Crab and Mushroom Ramekins

100g (4oz) very small button mushrooms
40g (1½oz) butter
salt and pepper
100g (4oz) crabmeat
300ml (½pt) Cheese Sauce (see Menu 18)
25g (1oz) cheese

To garnish
chopped parsley
paprika

Salami Platter

350g (12oz) various kinds of salami

To garnish
watercress or lettuce

Mixed Salad

salad ingredients (see method)
French Dressing (see Menu 34)

Peasant Girl in a Veil

900g (2lb) cooking apples
4tbspn water
75-100g (3-4oz) caster sugar
175g (6oz) bread (preferably rye or wholemeal)
100g (4oz) butter (preferably unsalted)
75-100g (3-4oz) sugar (preferably Demerara)

For the topping
150ml (¼pt) double cream
50g (2oz) plain chocolate

To Freeze Ahead

Crab and Mushroom Ramekins in dishes suitable for reheating in an oven or microwave cooker.
Peasant Girl in a Veil: freeze apple purée and fried crumb mixture separately; make dessert when defrosted.

Menu 14	Crab and Mushroom Ramekins
Serves 4	Salami Platter – Mixed Salad
	Peasant Girl in a Veil

Crab and Mushrooms Ramekins

Wipe the mushrooms and trim the base of the stalks. Heat the butter in a pan. Cook the mushrooms until just tender. Spoon most of the mushrooms into 4 individual oven-proof dishes; save 4 for garnish. Season lightly and top with the crabmeat, then the sauce. Grate the cheese and sprinkle over the sauce. Heat for 10-15 minutes towards the top of a moderately hot oven, 200°C, 400°F, Gas Mark 6, or under a moderate grill, or for 3-4 minutes in a microwave cooker. Top with the 4 mushrooms and a border of parsley. Dust with paprika. Serve with a small spoon and fork.

Salami Platter

Arrange the meats on a dish in a border of watercress or lettuce.

Mixed Salad

The salad should include tomatoes and cucumber to give a refreshing flavour after the rather rich hors d'oeuvre. Be generous with the mustard in the dressing (see Menu 34).

Peasant Girl in a Veil

Peel and thinly slice the apples. Put into a pan with the water and caster sugar and cook until a thick smooth purée. Allow to cool. Make breadcrumbs from the bread. Heat the butter in a large frying pan, add the breadcrumbs and turn in the butter. Cook steadily until crisp; do not allow to become too brown. Leave the crumbs until cold, then blend in the sugar. Put a layer of one-third of the crumbs into an attractive serving dish. Top with half the apple purée, then half the remaining crumbs. Add the last of the apple purée, then cover with the crumbs. Whip the cream lightly. Spread or pipe over the top of the pudding. Grate the chocolate and sprinkle over the cream.

To Make Sunday Easier

1   Make Crab and Mushroom Ramekins overnight.
2   Prepare salad ingredients.
3   Cook apple and crumb mixtures.

Foods Required

350g (12oz) salami, 100g (4oz) crabmeat, 165g (6½oz) butter, 150g (5oz) Cheddar cheese, 150ml (¼pt) double cream, 300ml (½pt) milk, 25g (1oz) flour, 75-100g (3-4oz) Demerara sugar, 75-100g (3-4oz) caster sugar, rye or wholemeal bread to give 175g (6oz) breadcrumbs, paprika, 50g (2oz) plain chocolate, 100g (4oz) very small mushrooms, 900g (2lb) cooking apples, lettuce, ingredients for Mixed Salad plus watercress, parsley, ingredients for French Dressing (see Menu 34).

Menu 14

Crab and Mushroom Ramekins; Peasant Girl in a Veil

A German hock would be a good accompaniment to the pâté and the main course. Apple juice would be a good choice for children.

Sweet and Sour Ham Pâté

350g (12oz) cooked lean ham
100g (4oz) butter
2tbspn chopped parsley
8 gherkins
6 rings canned pineapple
6 black olives (optional)
2tbspn dry sherry or single cream
few drops lemon juice
salt and pepper

Stuffed Chicken Breasts

For the stuffing
1 large onion
100g (4oz) mushrooms
50g (2oz) butter
50g (2oz) soft breadcrumbs
2tbspn chopped parsley
1 egg
salt and pepper

6 large chicken breasts

For the coating
25g (1oz) flour
1-2 eggs
75g (3oz) crisp breadcrumbs

For frying
75g (3oz) butter
1tbspn oil

To garnish
1-2 large lemons

Savoury Tomato Sauce

3 large tomatoes
1 medium onion
1 small dessert apple
40g (1½oz) butter or margarine
25g (1oz) flour
300ml (½pt) water
salt and pepper
pinch brown sugar
few drops Tabasco sauce
few drops soy sauce

Menu 15

Sweet and Sour Ham Pâté

Serves 6

Stuffed Chicken Breasts – Savoury Tomato Sauce
Parsley Potatoes – Harlequin Artichokes

Apricot Pudding – Lemon and Apricot Sauce

Sweet and Sour Ham Pâté

Mince the ham or put into a food processor or a liquidiser, or chop, then pound until smooth. Melt the butter, blend with the ham and parsley. Neatly dice, but not too finely, 6 gherkins, 4 pineapple rings and the olives. Stir into the ham mixture with the sherry or cream, lemon juice, salt and pepper. Spoon into one mould or individual moulds. Chill until firm. Garnish with small shapes cut from the remaining pineapple rings and gherkins. Serve with lettuce, brown or wholemeal toast or crispbread.

Stuffed Chicken Breasts

Peel and finely chop the onion; wipe and chop the mushrooms. Heat the butter and fry the vegetables until tender. Mix with the breadcrumbs, parsley, egg, salt and pepper. Slit the chicken breasts to make a deep 'pocket'; insert the stuffing. Blend a little salt and pepper with the flour, then coat the chicken. Beat the egg(s), brush over the floured chicken joints, then roll in the crisp breadcrumbs. Chill for 1 hour before frying.

Heat the butter and oil in a large frying pan. Fry the chicken steadily until brown on both sides; lower the heat and cook for a further 15 minutes until the chicken flesh is tender and the stuffing adequately heated. Drain on absorbent paper. Cut the lemon(s) into wedges; serve with the chicken.

Savoury Tomato Sauce

Skin and chop the tomatoes; the seeds can be removed if you do not intend to sieve the sauce after cooking. Peel and chop the onion and apple; grate these if the sauce is not being sieved. Heat the butter or margarine in a saucepan, cook the tomatoes, onion and apple until a soft purée; do not allow to discolour. Blend in the flour and cook over a low heat for 2-3 minutes, then add the water. Bring to the boil, stirring as you do so. Add salt, pepper, sugar and the sauces; simmer gently for a few minutes. Serve without sieving or rub through a sieve or put into a liquidiser or food processor, then reheat.

For Parsley Potatoes, see Menu 7.

Harlequin Artichokes

Scrape the artichokes to remove the peel. This vegetable discolours easily, so keep covered in cold water with half the lemon juice until ready to cook. Put into boiling salted water with the remaining lemon juice and cook steadily for about 20 minutes or until tender. Strain. Melt the butter in the pan, add the parsley, red pepper and artichokes. Stir gently until the artichokes are coated with the garnish.

Apricot Pudding

Cut the apricots into small pieces, put into a basin. Heat the water, pour over the apricots. Leave soaking overnight or for several hours, then strain; any liquid that remains can be incorporated into the sauce. Make fine crumbs of the macaroon biscuit and cake. Heat the milk. Beat together the eggs, egg yolks and sugar; add the hot, but not boiling, milk. Strain over the macaroon and cake crumbs. Grease a 1 litre (1¾pt) basin with butter; press the apricots on the base. Carefully pour the custard mixture over these. Cover with greased foil and steam or bake for 1½-1¾ hours as the Viennoise Pudding in Menu 5. Turn out and serve with Lemon and Apricot Sauce.

Lemon and Apricot Sauce

Halve the lemon, squeeze out the juice. Add sufficient water (or water and liquid left from soaking the apricots) to give 300ml (½pt). Blend with the arrowroot or cornflour. Put into a saucepan with the jam and sugar; stir over a low heat until thickened and clear.

To Make Sunday Easier

1 The Paté can be made several days beforehand if covered with melted butter (see below).
2 Prepare and coat chicken breasts on Saturday; chill well. Cook sauce ready for reheating.
3 Prepare ingredients for the Apricot Pudding.

Foods Required

350g (12oz) cooked lean ham, 6 large chicken breasts, 297g (11¾oz) butter, 1tbspn oil, 2tbspn single cream if not using sherry for the paté, 6-7 eggs (4-5 eggs and 2 yolks), 450ml (¾pt) milk, 50g (2oz) flour, 2tspn arrowroot or cornflour, bread to give 50g (2oz) soft breadcrumbs and 75g (3oz) crisp breadcrumbs, 75g (3oz) caster sugar plus pinch brown sugar, 4tbspn apricot jam, Tabasco sauce, soy sauce, 1 medium macaroon biscuit, 50g (2oz) sponge cake, 100g (4oz) dried apricots, 6 rings canned pineapple, 8 gherkins, 6 black olives, 2tbspn dry sherry if not using cream, 1 large and 1 medium onion, 3 large tomatoes, 675g (1½lb) potatoes, 450g (1lb) Jerusalem artichokes, 100g (4oz) mushrooms, 1 red pepper, parsley, 3-4 lemons, 1 small dessert apple.

Covering Pâtés

If paté is being kept for more than 1-2 days in the refrigerator it should be covered with a layer of melted butter. The butter excludes the air from the paté and helps to preserve it; also, of course, it prevents the paté from becoming dry. Heat 50g (2oz) unsalted butter, pour over the paté; allow to set.

Harlequin Artichokes

450g (1lb) Jerusalem artichokes
1tbspn lemon juice
salt

To garnish
25g (1oz) butter
2tbspn chopped parsley
2tbspn chopped red pepper

Apricot Pudding

100g (4oz) dried apricots
150ml (¼pt) water
1 medium macaroon biscuit
50g (2oz) sponge cake
450ml (¾pt) milk
2 eggs
2 egg yolks
50g (2oz) caster sugar
7g (¼oz) butter

Variation
The apricots tend to be fairly firm in this recipe. If softer fruit is required, use more water and simmer until tender, then strain and use as above.

Lemon and Apricot Sauce

1 large lemon
water (see method)
2tspn arrowroot or cornflour
4tbspn apricot jam
25g (1oz) sugar

To Freeze Ahead

Pâté: freeze for up to 2 weeks.
Stuffed Chicken Breasts: stuff, coat and open-freeze; do not cook before freezing.
Savoury Tomato Sauce freezes well; if it becomes slightly thinner when defrosted, simmer in open pan to thicken or blend in a little extra flour or cornflour.
Apricot Pudding can be frozen if single cream is substituted for milk. Lemon and Apricot Sauce freezes well.

Serve a dry white wine or dry sherry with the cold soup. A chilled Tio Pepe sherry would be ideal. A white or rosé wine is a good accompaniment to pork with an apple sauce.

Mushroom Vichyssoise
2 medium old potatoes
2 medium leeks
750ml (1¼pt) chicken stock
salt and pepper
150ml (¼pt) single cream
4tbspn white wine (optional) or extra stock
50g (2oz) small button mushrooms

To garnish
chopped chives

Roast Pork
Buy 2kg (4-4½lb) loin (if on bone) or 1.25kg (2½-3lb) (if boned) or 1.25kg (2½-3lb) fillet or part of leg
little oil or lard
salt (optional)

Apple Sauce
450g (1lb) cooking apples
2tbspn water
25-50g (1-2oz) sugar
25-50g (1-2oz) butter (optional)

Sage and Onion Stuffing
450g (1lb) onions
450ml (¾pt) water
salt and pepper
50-75g (2-3oz) butter
75-100g (3-4oz) soft breadcrumbs
3tspn fresh or 1½tspn dried sage
1 egg (optional)

Variation
Use margarine or shredded suet instead of butter.

Fan Roast Potatoes
675g (1½lb) medium potatoes
50-75g (2-3oz) fat

Spring Greens
675g (1½lb) spring greens
salt

Menu 16

Serves 6

Mushroom Vichyssoise

Roast Pork with Gravy — Apple Sauce
Sage and Onion Stuffing
Fan Roast Potatoes — Spring Greens

Linzertorte

Mushroom Vichyssoise
Peel and chop the potatoes. Dice the leeks; use only the tender part of the green stalks. Heat the stock, add the vegetables with a little salt and pepper, then cook for 15-20 minutes, or until tender. Do not over-cook for this spoils the colour. Sieve or put into a liquidiser or food processor to give a smooth purée. Cool, then blend in the cream and wine or extra stock. Wipe the mushrooms, cut into wafer-thin slices. Add to the soup. Top with the chives.

Roast Pork
In order to achieve good crackling, chine the skin (cut deeply at regular intervals). Brush with a very little oil or melted lard. A light sprinkling of salt encourages crisping, but is not popular with everyone. Do not cover pork when roasting. Pork can be cooked at Temperature 1 or 2, but you need Temperature 1 if roasting potatoes (see page 10). Serve with thickened gravy (see also page 10).

Apple Sauce
Peel and thinly slice the apples. Put into a saucepan with the other ingredients and simmer gently until a thick purée. Beat with a wooden spoon or sieve or liquidise until a smooth sauce. Serve hot or cold.

Sage and Onion Stuffing
Peel the onions, put into a saucepan with the water, a little salt and pepper, and simmer for 15 minutes or until nearly cooked. Lift the onions from the liquid, chop into small pieces. Melt the butter, add to the onions with the breadcrumbs and sage. Use the egg to bind or some of the liquid in which the onions were cooked. Season well. Put the stuffing into a dish, cover with greased foil and bake for 30-45 minutes, depending upon whether Temperature 1 or 2 is used. This stuffing is cooked within about 5 minutes in a microwave cooker on HIGH; cover with clingfilm before cooking.

Fan Roast Potatoes
Peel the potatoes, leave whole. Make cuts at 0.5cm (¼in) intervals in the potatoes; these cuts should extend over half-way through each potato. Heat the fat; turn the potatoes gently in the hot fat, but turn so the cut part of the potatoes are uppermost. Roast as shown in Menu 6.

Spring Greens
Shred the vegetable, wash in cold water and drain well just before cooking. Heat enough water to give a depth of about 4cm (1½in) in a good-

sized saucepan. Add a little salt. Add the prepared vegetable gradually to the boiling water. Cover the pan and cook quickly for approximately 5 minutes or until just tender, but never over-soft. Strain and serve.

Linzertorte

Grate the rind from the lemon; use only the yellow 'zest'. Sift the flour and cinnamon; add the sugar, ground almonds and lemon rind. Rub in the butter very quickly with the tips of the fingers so the mixture does not become over-sticky. Mix the egg yolks and vanilla essence, add to the flour mixture. Blend together with a knife, then with your finger tips until a soft dough. Wrap and chill for at least 1 hour to make it easier to handle. Grease a 24cm (9½in) flan dish. Knead the dough on a lightly floured surface. Put just under a quarter on one side to make a lattice over the filling. Press the remaining dough over the base and up the sides of the dish; spread the jam evenly over the base of the mixture. Roll out the reserved dough on a well-floured board to a rectangle about 20 × 8cm (8 × 3in); cut into 6 strips. Lift these strips carefully and lay them across the jam in a lattice pattern. Fold the edge of the pastry downwards to a depth of about 1cm (½in) to make a thicker border to the flan. Chill for 1 hour, then bake in the centre of a moderate oven, 180°C, 350°F, Gas Mark 4, for 35-40 minutes, until crisp and lightly browned. Allow to cool. Serve with ice-cream or cream.

To Make Sunday Easier

1 Prepare and chill soup if this is not frozen.
2 Cook Apple Sauce and Sage and Onion Stuffing.
3 Bake Linzertorte up to 48 hours ahead if this is not frozen; keep in an airtight tin.

Foods Required

Pork (see recipe), 185-235g (7-9oz) butter, 50-75g (2-3oz) fat, 150ml (¼pt) single cream plus cream if not serving ice-cream with Linzertorte, 3 eggs, 150g (5oz) plain flour plus flour for gravy, 110-135g (4-5oz) sugar, about 1tbspn oil or lard, white wine for soup, vanilla essence, 350g (12oz) raspberry jam, ground cinnamon, 50g (2oz) ground almonds, bread to give 75-100g (3-4oz) breadcrumbs, ice-cream if not serving cream with Linzertorte, 900g (2lb) old potatoes, 2 medium leeks, 50g (2oz) small button mushrooms, 675g (1½lb) spring greens, 450g (1lb) onions, chives, sage, 1 lemon, 450g (1lb) cooking apples.

Serving Coffee or Tea

A cup of coffee would be many people's choice after luncheon. If you are entertaining guests with whose tastes you are not completely familiar, then give them the alternative of coffee or tea—and of Indian or China tea—with milk or slices of lemon. A good cup of tea depends on boiling freshly drawn water, warming the tea-pot before making the tea and using good quality tea.

Hints on making coffee are given in Menu 22.

Linzertorte

1 lemon (rind only)
150g (5oz) plain flour
½tspn ground cinnamon
85g (3oz) caster sugar
50g (2oz) ground almonds
110g (4oz) unsalted butter
2 egg yolks★
¼tspn vanilla essence
350g (12oz) thick raspberry jam

★Save egg whites for meringues (see Menu 23).

Variation
The dough can be brushed with 1 egg yolk or 1tbspn single cream before baking to give a shine.

To Freeze Ahead

Mushroom Vichyssoise: do not add cream and wine until the soup is defrosted. The vegetable purée tends to separate during freezing; it improves the texture if it is sieved or liquidised again after thawing.
Apple Sauce, Stuffing and Linzertorte freeze well.

Smoked Trout with Herb Dressing

150ml (¼pt) mayonnaise (see Menu 34)
2tspn chopped parsley
2tspn chopped chives or dill
1tspn chopped fennel leaves
2-3tbspn horseradish cream
4 smoked trout

To garnish
lettuce, lemon slices and cucumber slices

Tournedos Rossini

50g (2oz) liver pâté (see Menu 33) or buy pâté
4 fillet steaks (tournedos) about 3.5cm (1½in) in thickness
75-100g (3-4oz) butter
salt and pepper
4 tomatoes
100g (4oz) button mushrooms
4 slices bread, size of tournedos

Lemon Syllabub

75g (3oz) loaf or icing sugar
2 large lemons
300ml (½pt) whipping or double cream
3tbspn white wine (optional)

To decorate
little grated lemon rind

To Freeze Ahead

The main dishes in this menu are not suitable for freezing, but both smoked trout and steaks freeze well. Cook steaks without defrosting.

Successful Grilled Steaks

1 Always pre-heat the grill.
2 Be generous with the amount of butter used in cooking.
3 Serve as soon as cooked.

Menu 17

Serves 4

Smoked Trout with Herb Dressing

Tournedos Rossini with Tomatoes and Mushrooms
Fried Potatoes – Green Salad

Lemon Syllabub

Smoked Trout with Herb Dressing

Blend the mayonnaise, herbs and horseradish cream together. Put the trout on a bed of lettuce, garnish with the lemon and cucumber slices.

Tournedos Rossini

Cut the pâté into 4 rounds or squares; chill well. If the butcher has not made the tournedos, form each fillet into a neat round with the palms of both hands; secure with fine string or cocktail sticks. Melt just over half the butter, season lightly. Pre-heat the grill. Brush one side of the steaks with some of the melted butter; cook, turn and brush on the second side with more butter. If cooking steaks of the thickness given (children may want thinner steaks), allow: under-done (rare) steaks, 2-3 minutes on either side; medium-done steaks, 2-3 minutes on either side, then 3-4 minutes on a lower heat; well-done steaks, 2-3 minutes on either side, then 6-7 minutes on a lower heat.

Brush the tomatoes and mushrooms with any melted butter left over, cook with the steaks. If the grill pan is not sufficiently large to accommodate vegetables and meat, cook the vegetables first; keep hot while cooking the steaks. Heat the remaining butter in a frying pan, cook the bread on either side until crisp and brown. Put on to a hot dish. Remove string or cocktail sticks from the steaks, lift on to the fried bread, top with the pâté. Serve with tomatoes and mushrooms.

For Fried Potatoes, see Menu 30; for Green Salad see Menu 37.

Lemon Syllabub

Rub loaf sugar over the lemons until all the yellow 'zest' is absorbed, then crush the sugar. If using icing sugar grate the 'zest' from the lemons. Avoid any white pith. Halve the fruit, squeeze out 4tbspn juice. Whip the cream until it holds its shape. Gradually whisk in the sugar, lemon rind and juice and wine. Spoon into 4 glasses; chill well and top with the lemon rind.

To Make Sunday Easier

Prepare dressing for trout and make Lemon Syllabub.

Foods Required

4 tournedos, 4 smoked trout, 50g (2oz) liver pâté or ingredients as in Menu 33, 75-100g (3-4oz) butter, oil or fat for frying, 300ml (½pt) whipping or double cream, 75g (3oz) loaf or icing sugar, 4 slices bread, 150ml (¼pt) mayonnaise (see Menu 34), horseradish cream, 3tbspn white wine, 4 tomatoes, 100g (4oz) mushrooms, 450g (1lb) potatoes, ingredients for Green Salad (see Menu 37) plus lettuce and piece cucumber, parsley, chives or dill, fennel, 3-4 lemons.

Menu 16
Linzertorte

A fruity red wine or chilled rosé wine or beer would be good with the pasta dish.

Stuffed Cucumber Salad

1 large cucumber
1tbspn lemon juice or white
  wine vinegar
1tbspn salad oil
salt and pepper
1 small red pepper
few spring onions
100-175g (4-6oz) peeled prawns
3tbspn mayonnaise (see Menu
  34)
1tbspn chopped parsley
1 lettuce

Lasagne al Forno

*For the Bolognese (meat)
  Sauce*
50g (2oz) mushrooms
1 medium onion
1 medium carrot
1-2 garlic cloves
25g (1oz) butter
1tbspn oil
350g (12oz) minced beef
300ml (½pt) beef stock
3-4tbspn tomato purée
1 bay leaf
1-2tbspn chopped parsley
1 wine glass red wine
salt and pepper

For the Cheese Sauce
40g (1½oz) butter or margarine
40g (1½oz) flour
450ml (¾pt) milk
1tspn made mustard
salt and pepper
100-175g (4-6oz) Gruyère or
  Cheddar cheese

225g (8oz) lasagne
50g (2oz) Gruyère or Cheddar
  cheese or 25g (1oz) Parmesan
  cheese, grated

Variation
Use only 300ml (½pt) Cheese
Sauce.

Green Salad

selection of the ingredients
  given in Menu 37
French Dressing (see Menu 34)

Menu 18   Stuffed Cucumber Salad

Serves 6   Lasagne al Forno – Green Salad

Pineapple – Vanilla Ice-cream

Stuffed Cucumber Salad

The cucumber can be peeled—this is advisable if the peel is tough. Cut into 5cm (2in) pieces; halve these lengthways. Remove the centre from each portion, chop finely, put on one side. Blend together the lemon juice or vinegar, oil, salt and pepper. Spoon over the pieces of cucumber and leave for 1 hour. Finely chop the pepper, discard core and seeds; finely chop the onions. Pour off any surplus dressing from the cucumber and blend this with the prawns, mayonnaise, half the pepper, all the onions and the chopped cucumber. Season to taste. Spoon into the cucumber shells; top with the chopped parsley and remaining red pepper. Serve on a bed of lettuce.

Lasagne al Forno

Make the meat sauce first. Wipe and chop the mushrooms; peel and grate or chop the onion and carrot; peel and crush the garlic. Heat the butter and oil in a saucepan, add the vegetables and cook gently for 3-4 minutes. Add the beef, stir well until the small particles of meat are well separated; this is important for a smooth sauce. Add the rest of the ingredients, bring to simmering point, cover the pan and simmer steadily for 35-45 minutes. Lift the lid after 25-30 minutes and check the amount of liquid in the pan. Keep the saucepan uncovered for a short time so any excess liquid can evaporate. Stir well during this period. Remove the bay leaf.

Heat the butter or margarine for the Cheese Sauce, stir in the flour, then gradually blend in the milk. Bring to the boil, add the seasoning, then stir over a low heat until thickened. Grate the cheese, add to the sauce; do not cook again as the cheese will melt in the hot sauce.

Bring at least 2.4 litres (4pt) water to the boil, add 1tspn salt, put in the lasagne and cook for 15 minutes, or as directed on the packet. Drain—you can rinse in cold water if desired. Allow the lasagne to dry in the air for a short time. Put a layer of lasagne into an oven-proof dish, top with a layer of the meat sauce, then a little Cheese Sauce, more lasagne, more meat and Cheese Sauce. End with the remaining lasagne and Cheese Sauce, then top with the grated cheese. Heat in the centre of a moderate oven, 180°C, 350°F, Gas Mark 4, for approximately 30 minutes.

Green Salad

Choose ingredients not used in the Cucumber Salad—add a rather acid-flavoured dressing (made by using less oil than the classic proportions) to balance the rather rich taste of the lasagne mixture.

Pineapple

Cut the pineapple into slices; cut away the skin with kitchen scissors; do this over a basin so no juice is wasted. Cut out the hard centre core from each slice with an apple corer. Arrange the pineapple rings on a flat dish with the attractive crest of leaves on top. Spoon any juice over the fruit.

Vanilla Ice-cream

Put the eggs into a mixing bowl. Sift the icing sugar into the eggs, add the vanilla essence. Whisk until thick and creamy; you should be able to see the trail of the whisk in the mixture. Whip the cream in a separate basin until it stands in peaks; whipping cream makes a less rich ice-cream. Fold the cream into the egg mixture. Spoon into a container and place in the freezing compartment of the refrigerator or in a freezer. There is no need to alter the cold control in a modern 3-star refrigerator or in a freezer when freezing ice-cream. This particular recipe does not need whisking during freezing.

If using evaporated milk, boil the can of milk in water to cover for 15 minutes; open carefully while hot. Dissolve 1tspn gelatine in 2tbspn water over a pan of hot water. Blend with the hot evaporated milk. Chill well and whip.

To Make Sunday Easier

1   Prepare French Dressing (see Menu 34); put in screw-topped jar. Prepare salad ingredients; put in salad container in refrigerator.
2   Make Lasagne al Forno the day beforehand ready for reheating.
3   Make and freeze the ice-cream.

Foods Required

350g (12oz) minced beef, 100-175g (4-6oz) peeled prawns, 65g (2½oz) butter, 175-225g (6-8oz) Gruyère or Cheddar cheese, 300ml (½pt) whipping or double cream (or unsweetened full-cream evaporated milk), 2 large eggs, 450ml (¾pt) milk, 40g (1½oz) flour, 50g (2oz) icing sugar, vanilla essence, 225g (8oz) lasagne, 3tbspn mayonnaise (see Menu 34), 3-4tbspn tomato purée, 1tbspn oil plus oil and white wine vinegar or lemon juice for salad and dressing, few tbspn red wine, made mustard, 1 small red pepper, few spring onions, 1 large cucumber, 1 medium onion, 1 medium carrot, 1-2 garlic cloves, lettuce, 50g (2oz) mushrooms, ingredients for Green Salad (see Menu 37), parsley, bay leaf, 1 pineapple.

Cooking Pasta

The recipe indicates the minimum amount of water that should be used when cooking lasagne or any type of pasta; this prevents the strands sticking together. Always make sure the salted water is boiling before adding the pasta and keep the water at boiling point throughout the cooking period.

Rinsing pasta is not essential, but this makes it less sticky. If you want to serve the pasta immediately after cooking, rinse in boiling water, then strain. If the pasta is to be reheated as in Lasagne al Forno you can rinse it in cold water, then strain it.

Pineapple

1 medium fresh pineapple

Variations
1 Pineapple Basket: cut the pineapple as for Melon and Strawberry Basket described in Menu 24.
2 Use canned pineapple rings.
3 Sprinkle the pineapple with a little kirsch.

Vanilla Ice-cream

2 large eggs
50g (2oz) icing sugar
¼tspn vanilla essence
300ml (½pt) whipping or
   double cream

Variation
Use unsweetened full-cream evaporated milk instead of cream.

To Freeze Ahead

Lasagne al Forno can be frozen for up to 3 months. Cook the pasta only lightly if planning to freeze the dish and make certain it is well covered with the sauces before freezing so it will not become dry. If the food is frozen in an oven-proof dish, allow to stand for a time at room temperature before putting into the oven. If you use a flame-proof dish there is no need for this to stand before the food is reheated in the oven. Take care to use a very low heat to begin with so the sauces gradually melt; this prevents the food drying, or even scorching, in the dish.

A microwave cooker is an ideal method of defrosting and then reheating pasta dishes. Ice-cream can be frozen in the freezing compartment of a refrigerator or in a freezer. Use within 3 months.

Serve chilled white wine with the soup and fish dish.

French Onion Soup
350g (12oz) onions
1-2 garlic cloves
40g (1½oz) butter
900ml (1½pt) really good beef stock
salt and pepper
4 rounds French bread
4tbspn grated Gruyère cheese

Fish Pie
50g (2oz) butter
40g (1½oz) flour
300ml (½pt) milk
150ml (¼pt) single cream
350g (12oz) cooked white fish
225g (8oz) cooked smoked fish
50g (2oz) peeled prawns
2tbspn chopped parsley
salt and pepper
Creamed Potatoes (see Menu 7)

Celeriac au Gratin
1 large or 2 small celeriac
few drops white malt vinegar or lemon juice
salt
squeeze lemon juice
40g (1½oz) butter
3-4tbspn soft breadcrumbs

Burgundy Pears
8 small firm pears
450ml (¾pt) water
150ml (¼pt) Burgundy red wine
50g (2oz) caster sugar
3tbspn redcurrant jelly
block ice-cream (or see Menu 18)

To Freeze Ahead
French Onion Soup: cook lightly before freezing.
Fish Pie freezes well.
Celeriac au Gratin: cook lightly before freezing.

Menu 19	French Onion Soup
Serves 4	Fish Pie with Celeriac au Gratin
	Burgundy Pears

French Onion Soup
Peel and chop the onions and garlic. Heat the butter, fry the onions and garlic for 5 minutes. Add the stock, salt and pepper. Cover the pan, simmer for 15-20 minutes. Top with the bread and grated cheese.

Fish Pie
Heat the butter, stir in the flour, cook for 2-3 minutes, then add the milk and cream. Bring to the boil, stir as the sauce thickens. Add the flaked white and smoked fish, prawns, parsley, salt and pepper to taste. Put into a pie dish, top with the creamed potatoes. Bake for 35 minutes in the centre of a moderate oven, 180°C, 350°F, Gas Mark 4.

Celeriac au Gratin
Peel and cut the celeriac into 0.5cm (½in) slices; halve each slice. Drop the prepared vegetable into cold water with the vinegar or lemon juice, drain, then cook in boiling salted water with a squeeze of lemon juice to keep it white. Cook for 12 minutes, drain, pat on absorbent paper. Melt the butter. Pack the celeriac into an oven-proof dish, brush each layer with butter, top with breadcrumbs and remaining butter. Bake for 30 minutes towards the top of a moderate oven.

Burgundy Pears
Peel and core the pears, but keep them whole. Heat the water, wine and sugar in a pan, add the pears and cook for 1 hour until tender. Lift out of the pan, add the redcurrant jelly, boil until only 300ml (½pt). Spoon over and around the fruit. Serve with ice-cream.

To Make Sunday Easier
1 Make the soup for Sunday; grate the cheese for the topping.
2 Prepare the fish Pie for the oven. Prepare the celeriac dish.
3 Cook the pears; they are nicer if they stand for 24 hours.

Foods Required
350g (12oz) white fish, 225g (8oz) smoked fish, 50g (2oz) peeled prawns, 200g (7oz) butter, 40g (1½oz) Gruyère cheese, 150ml (¼pt) single cream, 300ml (½pt) plus 3tbspn milk, block vanilla ice-cream or ingredients as in Menu 18, 40g (1½oz) flour, 50g (2oz) caster sugar, 3tbspn redcurrant jelly, 150ml (¼pt) Burgundy red wine, white malt vinegar, French bread to give 4 rounds plus bread to give 3-4tbspn breadcrumbs, 350g (12oz) onions, 1-2 garlic cloves, 1 large or 2 small celeriac, 450-675g (1-1½lb) potatoes, parsley, 1 lemon, 8 small pears.

Menu 22
Sardine Niçoise; Noisettes of Lamb with Paloise Sauce, Hot Potato Salad, Cucumber and Chicory Salad; Armagnac Apple Flan

Serve a dry white wine with the
fish mousse. This wine could also
be served with the duckling,
although most people prefer a
more flavoursome red wine, such
as a good Burgundy.

Smoked and Fresh Salmon Mousse

350g (12oz) fresh salmon
  (weight without skin and
  bones)
little oil
salt and pepper
1tbspn lemon juice
3tbspn fish stock or white
  wine or white vermouth
15g (½oz) gelatine
300ml (½pt) yoghurt
2tbspn thick mayonnaise (see
  Menu 34)
1tbspn tomato purée
100g (4oz) smoked salmon
2 egg whites

To garnish
lettuce
cucumber slices
lemon slices

Roast Duckling

2 young duckling
2tbspn melted butter

Variation
Serve the ducklings traditional
style with Apple Sauce and
Sage and Onion Stuffing (see
Menu 16).

Apricot Sauce

450g (1lb) apricots
150ml (¼pt) water
1tbspn lemon juice
50g (2oz) sugar
300ml (½pt) duck stock (see
  method)
3 level tspn arrowroot or
  cornflour
salt and pepper
1-2tbspn apricot brandy

Menu 20	Smoked and Fresh Salmon Mousse
Serves 6	Roast Duckling with Apricot Sauce
	Rillette of Duck
	Mashed Turnips – Mange Tout Peas
	Citrus Fruit Salad

Smoked and Fresh Salmon Mousse

If you intend using fish stock rather than white wine or vermouth, do not cook as instructed in Menu 24, but place the fish into boiling water, add a few drops of oil, a little salt, pepper and half the lemon juice; poach gently for about 8 minutes or until cooked. Drain and flake finely while still warm. Measure out 3tbspn of the fish stock or the wine or vermouth. Put this into a bowl, stand over a pan of very hot water. Sprinkle the gelatine on top of the liquid and allow to dissolve. If you have a microwave cooker you can use this very successfully for cooking both the fish and for dissolving the gelatine (follow manufacturer's instructions). Allow the gelatine mixture to cool slightly, add the rest of the lemon juice, the yoghurt, mayonnaise and tomato purée. Fold in the salmon and allow the mixture to chill until it begins to stiffen slightly.

Meanwhile, finely chop the smoked salmon, whisk the egg whites until stiff; fold the salmon and then the egg whites into the mixture. Spoon into a 1 litre (1¾pt) oiled mould and allow to set. Turn out and garnish with the lettuce, cucumber and lemon slice.

Roast Duckling

Simmer the giblets of the birds in water to cover. Add a little salt and pepper, but do not over-season. Cook for about 45 minutes, then strain the liquid. The cooked giblets can be made into a rillette and served on neat rounds of toast as a garnish to the dish. The liquid must be very clear for the sauce.

Frozen ducklings must be defrosted completely before cooking. It is better to roast these at the lower temperature (see page 10). As the skin tends to be rather moist after defrosting, dry well and brush with melted butter. Butter or additional fat is quite unnecessary when cooking fresh duckling. Fresh birds can be cooked at either Temperature 1 or 2, but weigh each duckling carefully and calculate the total cooking time. Put the birds in the hottest part of the oven and roast for 30 minutes; lift the tin from the oven. Prick the birds very lightly with a fine skewer or fork. If you prick too firmly, the excess fat does not spurt out of the bird, but tends to soak into the flesh. Return the ducklings to the oven and continue cooking, then lift on to a hot serving dish and keep hot while preparing the sauce. Strain 2tbspn of fat from the roasting tin into a saucepan for the sauce.

Apricot Sauce

Halve the apricots; remove, but do not discard, the stones. Heat the water, lemon juice and sugar, add the apricots and stones and simmer very gently for a few minutes. Strain the syrup from the fruit and stones. Slice the majority of the lightly cooked apricots, but keep just a

46

few halves to garnish the ducklings when served. Blend the duck stock with the arrowroot or cornflour. Put into the saucepan with the liquid from cooking the apricots. Stir over a low heat until thickened and clear. Add salt and pepper to taste, then the sliced apricots and apricot brandy, and heat gently.

Rillette of Duck

Remove the flesh from the cooked neck of the ducklings; dice the cooked liver and hearts very finely; discard the stomachs. Melt the butter. Put the cooked giblets, butter and stock into a food processor, switch on until smoothly blended, then add the salt, pepper, brandy or sherry. This can be served instead of pâté with toast or used as a garnish on rounds of toast for the Roast Duckling. The 'bite' of the rillette makes a pleasing contrast to the sweet sauce. Top each serving of rillette with a cocktail onion and olive.

Mashed Turnips

The French often serve duckling in a border of cooked sliced young turnips, but mashed turnips are an equally good alternative. Peel and dice the turnips, cook steadily in salted water, strain, mash and beat in the butter and any extra seasoning required. A little grated nutmeg may be added.

Mange Tout Peas

Wash the pods; trim any tiny pieces of stalk from the ends. Cook steadily in a very little salted water until tender. Strain and toss in the butter.

Citrus Fruit Salad

Cut away the rind and white pith from the fruit. Cut the top 'zest' from 1 orange and 2 tangerines into thin matchstick strips. Put the water or water and wine and strips of peel into a saucepan. Simmer until the peel is tender and the liquid reduced to 150ml (¼pt). Stir in the sugar. Slice the fruit, remove any pips. Put into a serving dish. Halve and stone the dates, chop the walnuts and sprinkle over the fruit. Chill before serving.

To Make Sunday Easier

1   Allow about 36 hours for the duckling to defrost. Simmer giblets; strain stock for gravy; make rillette.
2   Make the mousse on Saturday so it has time to set.

Foods Required

2 duckling, 350g (12oz) fresh salmon, 100g (4oz) smoked salmon, 175g (7oz) butter plus butter for toast, little oil, 2 eggs (whites only used), 300ml (½pt) yoghurt, 100-125g (4-5oz) sugar, 15g (½oz) gelatine, 3tspn arrowroot or cornflour, 2tbspn mayonnaise (see Menu 34), 1tbspn tomato purée, nutmeg (optional), bread for toast, 75g (3oz) dessert dates, 25g (1oz) walnuts, 150ml (¼pt) sweet white wine or vermouth, 1-2tbspn apricot brandy, 1-2tbspn brandy or sweet sherry, cocktail onions, black or green olives, 675-900g (1½-2lb) turnips, 675-900g (1½-2lb) mange tout peas, lettuce, piece cucumber, 450g (1lb) apricots, 3 lemons, 3 large oranges, 4 tangerines, 1 small grapefruit.

Variations
1 Use less sugar and add 2tbspn redcurrant jelly with the stock.
2 Use canned apricots; add a little lemon juice to syrup and boil down until 150ml (¼pt).

Rillette of Duck
cooked giblets from 2 duckling
50g (2oz) butter
2tbspn duck stock
salt and pepper
1-2tbspn brandy or sweet sherry

toast (see method)

To garnish
cocktail onions
black or green olives

Mashed Turnips
675-900g (1½-2lb) turnips
salt and pepper
50g (2oz) butter
nutmeg (optional)

Mange Tout Peas
675-900g (1½-2lb) mange tout peas
salt
25g (1oz) butter

Citrus Fruit Salad
3 large oranges
4 tangerines
1 small grapefruit
300ml (½pt) water or 150ml (¼pt) water and 150ml (¼pt) sweet white wine
50-75g (2-3oz) granulated or caster sugar
75g (3oz) dessert dates
25g (1oz) walnuts

To Freeze Ahead
Smoked and Fresh Salmon Mousse freezes perfectly in spite of containing mayonnaise which is often unsatisfactory. Apricot Sauce and Rillette of Duck freeze well. Obviously the latter means thawing out frozen duckling giblets to make stock and the rillette.

Consommé

1kg (2lb) shin of beef
3 litres (5pt) beef stock prepared from beef bones
salt and pepper
2 bay leaves
2 egg whites plus egg shells
  (optional)
150-300ml (¼-½pt) dry sherry

Creamed Scallops

8 scallops
300ml (½pt) milk
salt and pepper
50g (2oz) butter
25g (1oz) flour
25g (1oz) soft breadcrumbs

Variation
Pipe Creamed or Duchesse
Potatoes (see Menus 7 and 49)
around the edge of 8 scallop
shells. Spoon the cooked fish
mixture into the potato border,
add the topping and heat.

Fried Courgettes

450g (1lb) courgettes
25g (1oz) flour
salt and pepper

For frying
2-3tbspn oil

Variation
Coat the courgettes in flour,
then beaten egg and crisp
breadcrumbs, and deep fry.

Snowdon Pudding

1 lemon or 1 orange
75g (3oz) soft breadcrumbs
25g (1oz) flour
50g (2oz) shredded suet or
  margarine
75g (3oz) light brown or caster
  sugar
2tbspn lemon or orange
  marmalade
1 egg
100g (4oz) seedless raisins
50g (2oz) glacé cherries
15g (½oz) butter

Menu 21	Consommé
Serves 4	Creamed Scallops — Rice
	Fried Courgettes
	Snowdon Pudding — Marmalade Sauce

Consommé

Dice the meat, add the stock together with the salt, pepper and bay leaves. Simmer for 1½-2 hours. The liquid is reduced considerably during this period. Strain through several thicknesses of muslin. If the consommé still contains tiny particles of meat, return to the pan; lightly whisk the egg whites and add these, with the shells, to the soup. Simmer for a further 15-20 minutes and you will find that the egg shells and whites gather these tiny pieces of meat. Strain again. Add the sherry and taste the soup; add more salt and pepper if necessary. The quantity given in this recipe would serve at least 8 people, but it is worthwhile making a good quantity of consommé and using it in various ways, or freezing as instructions below.

Creamed Scallops

Lift the scallops off the shells; if there is any liquid under the fish, pour this into the saucepan; add the milk with a very little salt and pepper. The scallops can be left whole or cut into pieces. Put the fish into the milk, bring to simmering point, then simmer gently until tender; this takes 5-7 minutes depending on the size. Lift the fish from the liquid with a perforated spoon. Heat half the butter in a saucepan, stir in the flour, cook gently for 2-3 minutes, then gradually blend in the milk in which the scallops were cooked. Bring the sauce to the boil stirring all the time; cook until thickened. Add the scallops with any salt and pepper required. Spoon into 4 flame-proof dishes. Melt the remaining butter, mix with the breadcrumbs and sprinkle over the fish mixture. Heat under the grill or warm in the oven.

Method for cooking rice, see Menu 32.

Fried Courgettes

Wash and dry the courgettes. Cut off the tough ends, then cut the vegetables into 0.5cm (¼in) slices. Lay flat on absorbent paper, cover with more absorbent paper and leave for a short time. This means that the paper absorbs some of the excess liquid from the watery vegetable. Blend the flour with a little salt and pepper, then coat the slices. Heat the oil and fry the courgettes until golden and tender on one side. Turn and fry on the second side. Drain on absorbent paper.

Snowdon Pudding

Grate the rind from the lemon or orange. Halve the fruit, squeeze out the juice and save this to add to the sauce. Mix together the bread-crumbs, flour and suet; if using margarine, melt this and add to the flour and breadcrumbs. Stir in the sugar, grated rind, marmalade, egg, half the raisins and half the cherries. Grease a 1 litre (1¾pt) basin with the butter. Press the remaining raisins and cherries on the base of this. Spoon the breadcrumb mixture into the basin; cover well. Steam for 1¾-2 hours over steadily, but not rapidly, boiling water. Serve with Marmalade Sauce (below).

Marmalade Sauce
Put the marmalade into a saucepan. Blend the arrowroot or cornflour with the orange or lemon juice and sufficient water to make 150ml (¼pt). Add to the marmalade; stir over a low heat until thickened and smooth.

To Make Sunday Easier
1   Make consommé a day or so beforehand if this is not being frozen.
2   Prepare the Creamed Scallops; put into the individual dishes, add the topping. On Sunday heat in the oven.
3   Make the pudding; do not cook this; cover and put into the refrigerator. Prepare the sauce ready to heat on Sunday.

Foods Required
1kg (2lb) shin of beef, 8 scallops, 65g (2½oz) butter, 50g (2oz) shredded suet or margarine, 3 eggs (2 whites only used), 300ml (½pt) milk, 75g (3oz) flour, 75g (3oz) light brown or caster sugar, 3tbspn oil, bread to give 100g (4oz) breadcrumbs, 225g (8oz) lemon or orange marmalade, 50g (2oz) glacé cherries, 100g (4oz) seedless raisins, 1tspn arrowroot or cornflour, 175g (6oz) long grain rice, 150-300ml (¼-½pt) dry sherry, 2 bay leaves, 450g (1lb) courgettes, 1 lemon or orange.

Marmalade Sauce
175g (6oz) marmalade
1tspn arrowroot or cornflour
orange or lemon juice (see method, Snowdon Pudding)
water (see method)

To Freeze Ahead
Consommé: sensible to cook a large amount, but to freeze in family-sized packs.
Creamed Scallops: since it toughens scallops, like other shellfish, to cook twice, it is better not to freeze the completed dish; raw scallops freeze well.
Snowdon Pudding: freeze before or after cooking.

49

Sardines Niçoise
4 large tomatoes
1 small onion
2 garlic cloves
1¼tbspn oil
2tbspn chopped parsley
salt and pepper
8 small fresh or frozen sardines
2tspn lemon juice
few black olives

Variation
Use sprats if sardines are not available.

Noisettes of Lamb with Paloise Sauce
8 loin or best end of neck lamb
  cutlets

For the sauce
75g (3oz) butter
2 egg yolks*
salt and pepper
½tspn French mustard
1tbspn lemon juice
1tbspn finely chopped mint

Hot Potato Salad
450g (1lb) very small new
  potatoes
salt

Dressing for both salads
2tbspn olive or salad oil
2tbspn white wine vinegar
2tbspn finely chopped fresh
  mixed herbs
salt and pepper

Garnish for Potato Salad
2-3tbspn coarsely chopped
  spring onions

Menu 22	Sardines Niçoise
Serves 4	Noisettes of Lamb with Paloise Sauce
	Hot Potato Salad—Cucumber and Chicory Salad
	Armagnac Apple Flan

Sardines Niçoise
Skin and deseed the tomatoes (concass), then chop into small pieces. Peel and grate the onion; peel and crush the garlic. Heat 1tbspn oil in a pan and fry the vegetables slowly until a thick purée. Add half the parsley, a little salt and pepper. Clean the sardines and remove the heads; brush with the remaining oil, sprinkle with lemon juice, salt and pepper. Grill for 6-7 minutes until tender. Put the tomato mixture on to a hot dish, top with the sardines, the remaining parsley and the olives.

Noisettes of Lamb with Paloise Sauce
Ask the butcher to bone and roll the cutlets (these are 'noisettes'). Grill steadily until tender.

To make the sauce, ensure that the butter is at room temperature. Whisk the egg yolks with the seasoning and lemon juice over a pan of hot, but not boiling, water until thick. Gradually whisk in the butter, then add the chopped mint. Put the noisettes on to a hot dish; remove the string from the sides. Top with the sauce and serve.

Note Many people avoid making whisked sauces, such as the Paloise Sauce above which is a derivation of Hollandaise Sauce (see Menu 47), because of the time necessary to stand and whisk the mixture. (Obviously a hand electric whisk makes the task quicker and easier.) You can, however, produce an excellent sauce very quickly using a liquidiser or food processor. Warm the lemon juice or vinegar slightly. Put the egg yolks and seasonings into the liquidiser goblet or food processor bowl. Cover and switch on for 2-3 seconds, add the warm vinegar or lemon juice, switch on again. Heat the butter to boiling point; do not let it discolour. Pour steadily over the egg-yolk mixture with the machine in operation.

If making mayonnaise in the liquidiser or food processor, as mentioned in Menu 51, put the egg yolks or whole eggs and seasonings into the goblet or bowl, cover and switch on for a few seconds, then steadily add the oil (which must be at room temperature) with the machine in operation. Lastly, add the lemon juice or vinegar.

Hot Potato Salad
Scrape the potatoes or cook in their skins if preferred. Boil steadily in boiling salted water, then strain. Blend the oil, vinegar, herbs and a little salt and pepper together. Toss the hot potatoes in half this dressing; top with the spring onions.

Cucumber and Chicory Salad

Shred the lettuce, put into a salad bowl. Slice the cucumber; divide each chicory head into 4 portions, arrange in the dish. Peel and dice the beetroot, put on top of the other ingredients. Toss with the remainder of the dressing just before serving.

Armagnac Apple Flan

Cream together the butter or margarine and sugar. Sift the flour into the mixture, add the egg yolk and just enough water to bind. Roll out thinly and line a 20cm (8in) flan dish. Bake 'blind' as described in Menu 26, but in view of the relatively high percentage of sugar check that the pastry does not become over-brown. Bake for approximately 20 minutes in the centre of a moderate oven, 190°C, 375°F, Gas Mark 5; lower the heat slightly after 12 minutes if necessary. The flan should be completely cooked before the filling is added.

Meanwhile, peel and thickly slice the apples; put into a large thick frying pan with half the armagnac, half the sugar and all the butter. Cook over a low heat, stirring well until the apples are just tender, but unbroken. They should turn an attractive golden colour.
To serve hot: keep both pastry and apples warm, put together at the last minute.
To serve cold: bake the flan earlier, allow to become quite cold; allow the apples to cool, then put together.

In each case, the finishing touch is given by warming together the remaining sugar, cinnamon and armagnac, then spooning this over the fruit the moment before serving.

To Make Sunday Easier

1   Prepare the tomato mixture for the Sardines Niçoise if not freezing this. Clean the sardines ready for cooking.
2   Make and bake the flan; poach the apples as the recipe. If serving the flan hot on Sunday, warm the pastry case for a few minutes; reheat the apples, then put these into the flan and complete the dish, as in the recipe.

Foods Required

8 loin or best end of neck lamb cutlets, 8 small fresh or frozen sardines, 175g (7oz) butter, 3½tbspn oil, cream if required to serve with flan, 3 eggs (yolks only used), 150g (5oz) plain flour, 190g (6½oz) sugar (can be all caster), 2 tbspn white wine vinegar, 1 liqueur glass armagnac, ground cinnamon, black olives, French mustard, ¼ large cucumber, 4 large tomatoes, 1 small onion, few spring onions, 2 garlic cloves, 1 small lettuce heart, 2 heads chicory, 1 small cooked beetroot, 450g (1lb) very small new potatoes, parsley, mint, mixed fresh herbs, 1 lemon, 675g (1½lb) Cox's dessert apples.

Cucumber and Chicory Salad

1 small lettuce heart
¼ large cucumber
2 heads chicory
1 small cooked beetroot

Armagnac Apple Flan

For the flan (fleur) pastry
75g (3oz) butter or margarine
40g (1½oz) caster sugar
150g (5oz) plain flour
1 egg yolk★
water to bind

★Use whites in meringues (see Menu 23).

For the filling
675g (1½lb) Cox's dessert apples
1 liqueur glass armagnac
150g (5oz) sugar
25g (1oz) butter
1tspn ground cinnamon

Variation
Use other brandy or calvados (apple liqueur).

To Freeze Ahead

Sardines Niçoise: while you can freeze the tomato mixture, cook the sardines just before serving the dish.
Paloise Sauce freezes well; when defrosted, whisk to lighten once more.
Armagnac Apple Flan: freeze cooked or uncooked pastry flan case; cook apples on Sunday to add to the pastry.

Making Good Coffee

Coffee should be made with water that is freshly drawn from the cold water system. Whatever method is chosen use 4 level tbspn ground coffee to each 600ml (1pt) water.

If using a percolator, drip-method or other type of coffee-maker, choose a medium ground coffee or as recommended by the manufacturer.

The luxury of Beef Stroganoff demands a very special red wine, such as a claret.

Salad Niçoise
3 eggs
175g (6oz) cooked new potatoes
175g (6oz) cooked French beans
¼ medium cucumber
4 medium tomatoes
200g (7oz) can tuna in oil
small can anchovy fillets
1 lettuce
4tbspn French Dressing (see Menu 34)
12 black olives

Beef Stroganoff
550-675g (1¼-1½lb) fillet steak
salt and pepper
2 medium onions
100g (4oz) button mushrooms
100g (4oz) butter
1tbspn flour
300ml (½pt) soured cream
1tbspn tomato purée
1tspn made mustard

225g (8oz) long grain rice
water
salt to taste

Courgettes and Cauliflower
450-675g (1-1½lb) courgettes
salt
25g (1oz) butter
1 medium cauliflower

Meringue Nests
3 eggs whites
175g (6oz) caster sugar
300ml (½pt) water
50g (2oz) granulated sugar
350-450g (¾-1lb) ripe fresh black cherries
2tbspn redcurrant jelly
150ml (¼pt) double cream

To Freeze Ahead
Not a suitable menu.

Menu 23

Serves 6

Salad Niçoise

Beef Stroganoff with Rice
Courgettes—Cauliflower

Meringue Nests with Black Cherries

Salad Niçoise
Hard-boil, shell and quarter the eggs; slice the vegetables. Drain and flake the tuna, drain the anchovies. Prepare the lettuce, put into the salad bowl, top with the other ingredients.

Beef Stroganoff
Cut the meat into narrow strips, season and leave for 1 hour. Peel and slice the onions, wipe and slice the mushrooms. Heat the butter in a frying pan, cook the onions until transparent; add the mushrooms and steak, fry for 2-3 minutes; blend in the flour, then the rest of the ingredients and cook for 5-10 minutes, according to personal taste.
Serve with rice, cooked as described in Menu 32.

Courgettes and Cauliflower
Wash the courgettes, cut into thin slices, discard tough ends. Cook in boiling salted water for 5 minutes, strain, top with butter. Divide cauliflower into florets, cook in boiling salted water for 5 minutes or until still 'nutty'; strain and serve.

Meringue Nests with Black Cherries
Oil a flat baking tray or use silicone (non-stick) paper on the tray. Whisk the egg whites until stiff; gradually beat in half the sugar, fold in the remainder. Spoon or pipe into nest shapes, as shown on page 53. Bake for about 2 hours, until firm, in a very cool oven, 90°-110°C, 200-225°F, Gas Mark ¼-½, then cool. Heat the water and sugar, poach the cherries for 3 minutes, drain. Heat the syrup and redcurrant jelly until 6tbspn remain. Whip the cream. Fill the meringues with the cherries, glaze and add cream just before serving.

To Make Sunday Easier
1 Prepare cooked salad ingredients, cover. Make dressing.
2 Bake meringue cases—they keep in an airtight tin for months.

Foods Required
550-675g (1¼-1½lb) fillet steak, 200g (7oz) canned tuna, small can anchovy fillets, 125g (5oz) butter, 150ml (¼pt) double cream, 300ml (½pt) soured cream, 6 eggs (only whites of 3 used), 1tbspn flour, 175g (6oz) caster sugar, 50g (2oz) granulated sugar, ingredients for French Dressing (see Menu 34), 225g (8oz) long grain rice, 12 black olives, 1tbspn tomato purée, 2tbspn redcurrant jelly, mustard, new potatoes and French beans (each to give 175g (6oz) when cooked), 4 medium tomatoes, ¼ cucumber, 1 lettuce, 100g (4oz) button mushrooms, 450-675g (1-1½lb) courgettes, 1 medium cauliflower, 2 medium onions, 350-450g (¾-1lb) fresh black cherries.

Menu 23
Meringue Nests with Black Cherries

Obviously, a very good dry white wine is the only partner to salmon. It would also blend well with the soup. To complement the Spanish soup, a Spanish white wine would be ideal. The Rioja or Penédes areas produce excellent white wine.

Gazpacho

water (see method)
1 medium cucumber
4 medium onions
1-2 garlic cloves
675g (1½lb) ripe tomatoes
2-4tbspn olive oil
1tbspn lemon juice or white
    wine vinegar
salt and pepper
75-100g (3-4oz) bread, weight
    without crusts
1 red pepper
1 green pepper

Poached Salmon Cutlets

4 salmon cutlets (darne), each
    about 150-175g (5-6oz)

For the Court Bouillon

Method 1
2 small carrots
1 small onion
1 stick of celery
900ml (1½pt) water
1 bay leaf
sprig of parsley
sprig of thyme
salt and pepper
3tbspn white wine or 1tbspn
    lemon juice

Method 2
1tbspn olive oil or melted
    butter
salt and pepper
squeeze of lemon juice

To garnish
lemon slices
cucumber slices

Menu 24

Serves 4

Gazpacho

Poached Salmon Cutlets—Hollandaise Sauce
New Potatoes—Cucumber and Mixed Salads

Melon and Strawberry Basket

Gazpacho

Put a jug of water into the refrigerator to become very cold. Peel the cucumber, onions and garlic. Put half the cucumber and 2 onions on one side. Finely chop the remaining onions, cucumber and the garlic. Skin the tomatoes, unless you intend sieving them, when the skins will be left behind in the sieve. Chop the tomatoes, mix with the cucumber and other chopped ingredients. Rub through a sieve, or pound together until a very smooth mixture, or put into a liquidiser or food processor and switch on until a smooth purée. Add a little of the chilled water to the liquidiser goblet or food processor bowl to make sure none of the thick mixture is wasted.

Pour the tomato mixture into a large chilled mixing bowl, then gradually blend in the oil—the amount depends upon personal taste. Add the lemon juice or vinegar, salt and pepper and enough chilled water to give a flowing consistency. Transfer the soup to a tureen or glass serving bowl; chill thoroughly.

Make the bread into fine crumbs, put into a small dish. Cut the remaining cucumber and onions into small neat dice; also dice the red and green peppers, discard the cores and seeds. Place these ingredients into separate small dishes and arrange around the container of soup. Each person helps themselves to their selected accompaniments.

Poached Salmon Cutlets

There are two ways of cooking salmon cutlets. The first is to put the fish into the liquid and simmer this, the second is to wrap each cutlet into a neat parcel of oiled or buttered paper and cook the fish in salted water. The latter method tends to keep the fish more moist.

Method 1 Peel and slice the carrots and onion, dice the celery. Put into a large wide pan—a fish kettle is, of course, ideal or a deep frying pan. Add 900ml (1½pt) water, the herbs, salt and pepper. Simmer for 30 minutes, strain, return to the pan, add the wine or lemon juice and bring to the boil. Place the fish into the Court Bouillon. Bring the liquid back to simmering point only—never let it boil once the fish has been added. Simmer the cutlets for approximately 7-8 minutes or until just tender. If you have thicker slices, ie about 2.5cm (1in), you need to simmer gently for about 10 minutes. If buying fish in a piece instead of cutlets, allow 10 minutes per 450g (1lb). Drain, put on to a serving dish and garnish (see below).

Method 2 Cut 4 large squares of greaseproof paper or use greaseproof paper bags. Spread the paper with the oil or melted butter (oil is better when serving salmon cold as butter gives a slightly 'cloudy' look to the outside of the fish, which does not matter when it is served hot). Place the fish on the paper or in the bag, add a little salt and pepper and squeeze of lemon juice, tie securely but carefully so the fish is not damaged. Put the parcels into boiling salted water. Time as above. Unwrap, drain, put on to a serving dish and garnish with lemon and cucumber slices.

Hollandaise Sauce
Make the sauce as the method described in Menu 47.

New Potatoes
Scrape the potatoes, or simply scrub and leave the skins on them. Cook steadily in boiling salted water until tender; add a sprig of mint for extra flavour, then strain. Melt the butter in the saucepan, add the parsley, then return the potatoes to the pan and turn in the butter and parsley.

Cucumber Salad
Slice the cucumber thinly. Put into a dish, add salt, pepper and a little vinegar. Leave to marinate for at least 1 hour.

Mixed Salad
It would be wise to avoid strongly flavoured ingredients, such as spring onions or those that have been used in the soup.

Melon and Strawberry Basket
Cut a thin slice lengthways from the melon. Spoon out and discard the seeds from the fruit. Either dice the melon pulp or cut into small balls with a vegetable scoop; keep the skin intact. Hull the strawberries, blend with the melon. Sweeten with a little sugar. Spoon back into the melon case. Add the sherry if desired. Chill well before serving.

To Make Sunday Easier
1   Make and chill Gazpacho unless this has been frozen, in which case bring out of freezer to allow time to defrost.
2   Prepare salad ingredients; put into salad container of refrigerator.

Foods Required
4 salmon cutlets, 150-225g (5-8oz) butter (if using butter in Method 2 for cooking salmon), cream (if serving with Melon and Strawberry Basket), 3 eggs (yolks only needed), 3-5tbspn olive oil, little sugar, bread to give 75-100g (3-4oz) breadcrumbs, little white wine vinegar, 2tbspn dry sherry (optional), 2 cucumbers, 4 onions, 1-2 garlic cloves, 675g (1½lb) ripe tomatoes, 1 red pepper, 1 green pepper, ingredients for Mixed Salad (see Menu 26), 450g (1lb) new potatoes, mint, bay leaf, thyme, parsley, 1 honeydew melon, 225g (8oz) small strawberries, 2 lemons to give 3tbspn lemon juice or white wine vinegar.

If using Method 1 for cooking salmon: 2 small carrots, 1 small onion, 1 stick celery, parsley, thyme, bay leaf, 3tbspn white wine or lemon juice.

Hollandaise Sauce
3 egg yolks
salt and pepper
2tbspn lemon juice or white wine vinegar
75-175g (3-6oz) butter

New Potatoes
450g (1lb) new potatoes
salt
sprig of mint
25g (1oz) butter
1-2tbspn chopped parsley

Cucumber Salad
½ large cucumber
salt and pepper
little white wine vinegar

Mixed Salad
See under method (see also Menu 26).

Melon and Strawberry Basket
1 honeydew melon
225g (8oz) small strawberries
little sugar
2tbspn dry sherry (optional)

To Freeze Ahead
Gazpacho: freeze smooth purée soup, but not the accompaniments except the breadcrumbs; the other accompaniments should be fresh and crisp. Hollandaise Sauce: prepare as recipe in Menu 47. Whisk as mixture cools, then freeze. Whisk well when defrosted to restore original light texture.

Freezing Eggs
Do not freeze whole or raw cooked eggs. Freeze left-over egg whites or yolks separately. Put egg whites into a suitable container, and mark number of egg whites.

Egg yolks should be lightly whisked and either seasoned or slightly sweetened.

Serve a light rosé wine or well-chilled lager with this meal.

Egg Mousse
15g (½oz) gelatine
2tbspn dry sherry
2tbspn water
6 eggs
4tbspn mayonnaise (see Menu 34)
½tbspn lemon juice
150ml (¼pt) whipping cream
salt and pepper
few drops Tabasco sauce

To garnish
cucumber slices

Lamb and Prune Casserole
175g (6oz) dried prunes
150ml (¼pt) water
25g (1oz) flour
salt and pepper
garlic salt
8 best end of neck lamb chops
12 small shallots or tiny onions
50g (2oz) fat
300ml (½pt) dry cider

New Potatoes and French Beans
450-675g (1-1½lb) new potatoes
450g (1lb) French beans
salt
mint
butter

Gooseberry Charlotte
450g (1lb) gooseberries
2tbspn water
75g (3oz) sugar
75g (3oz) butter or margarine
175g (6oz) coarse soft breadcrumbs
50-75g (2-3oz) sugar, preferably Demerara

To Freeze Ahead
Lamb and Prune Casserole freezes well for up to 3 months.
Gooseberry Charlotte: unwrap frozen pudding before reheating gently in oven.

Menu 25

Serves 4

Egg Mousse

Lamb and Prune Casserole
New Potatoes—French Beans—Green Salad

Gooseberry Charlotte with Cream

Egg Mousse
Sprinkle the gelatine on to the sherry and water, dissolve over hot water. Hard-boil 4 eggs; separate the remaining eggs. Whisk the yolks until thick. Blend with the warm gelatine liquid; cool, add the mayonnaise and lemon juice. Whip the cream, chop the hard-boiled eggs. Blend all the ingredients, except the egg whites, into the gelatine mixture, allow to stiffen slightly. Whisk the 2 egg whites, fold into the mixture. Spoon into individual dishes; when set, top with cucumber. Serve with a teaspoon and small fork.

Lamb and Prune Casserole
Soak the prunes in the water overnight. Blend the flour, salt, pepper and garlic salt; coat the chops. Peel the shallots or onions. Heat the fat in a frying pan, fry the shallots or onions until golden, lift into a casserole. Fry the chops for 4-5 minutes, add to the casserole. Heat the cider and prunes in the pan, spoon over the chops; cover the casserole. Cook for 1¼ hours in the centre of a moderate oven, 180°C, 350°F, Gas Mark 4.

Cook New Potatoes as in Menu 7 and French Beans as in Menu 43. For Green Salad, see Menu 37.

Gooseberry Charlotte
Top and tail the fruit; cook gently in the water and sugar until beginning to soften. Heat the butter or margarine in a large frying pan. Add the breadcrumbs, fry until golden. Stir in the remaining sugar. Put half the crumb mixture into a 1.2 litre (2pt) pie dish, top with the fruit purée, then the remaining crumbs. Bake for 30-35 minutes just above the centre of a moderate oven. Serve hot with cream.

To Make Sunday Easier
1 Make Egg Mousse on Saturday; garnish just before serving.
2 Cook Lamb and Prune Casserole; prepare salad ingredients.
3 Prepare gooseberries and crumb mixture; keep separately.

Foods Required
8 best end of neck lamb chops, 100g (4oz) butter, 50g (2oz) fat, 300ml (½pt) whipping cream, 6 eggs, 25g (1oz) flour, 75g (3oz) white sugar, 50-75g (2-3oz) Demerara sugar, 15g (½oz) gelatine, 4tbspn mayonnaise (see Menu 34), 175g (6oz) prunes, bread to give 175g (6oz) breadcrumbs, Tabasco sauce, garlic salt, 2tbspn dry sherry, 300ml (½pt) dry cider, 12 shallots or tiny onions, 450-675g (1-1½lb) new potatoes, 450g (1lb) French beans, ingredients for Green Salad (see Menu 37) plus cucumber, mint, 450g (1lb) gooseberries, lemon.

Menu 24
Gazpacho and Accompaniments

Genoese Flan

For the shortcrust pastry
175g (6oz) plain flour
pinch salt
85g (3oz) butter or
    margarine or cooking fat
    or use a mixture of fats
water to bind

For the filling
100g (4oz) Gruyère cheese
100g (4oz) cream cheese
3 eggs
2tbspn single cream or milk
1tbspn chopped parsley
1tspn chopped basil
salt and pepper

Galantine of Beef

4 rashers streaky bacon
0.75kg (1½lb) topside of beef
    or good quality chuck steak
225g (8oz) pork sausage-meat
½tspn fresh or pinch dried sage
1tbspn chopped parsley
2 eggs
4tbspn beef stock
salt and pepper

Variations
1 This is a good basic recipe which can be varied, eg use a mixture of beef and veal or beef and chicken and/or ham.
2 Put hard-boiled eggs in the centre of the uncooked mixture.
3 This galantine can be served hot with gravy or a sauce and hot vegetables.

Potato Salad

450g (1lb) old or new potatoes
salt
1tbspn salad oil
1tbspn white wine or malt
    vinegar
4tbspn mayonnaise (see Menu
    34)
2tbspn chopped parsley
2tbspn chopped chives

Menu 26	Genoese Flan
Serves 6	Galantine of Beef Potato Salad – Mixed Salad
	Lemon Sponge – Fresh Fruit
	Iced Coffee

Genoese Flan

Sift the flour and salt, rub in the fat until the mixture is like fine breadcrumbs. Add water to bind. Roll out and line a shallow 20cm (8in) flan dish or tin or use a flan ring on an upturned baking tray (this makes it easier to slide the cooked pastry off the tray). Bake 'blind' (see below) in the centre of a moderately hot oven, 200°C, 400°F, Gas Mark 6, for 15 minutes; do not allow to become too brown. Grate the cheese, blend with the cream cheese; gradually beat in the eggs, cream or milk and herbs, season well. Pour into the partially cooked pastry. Return to the centre of the oven for 30 minutes; lower the heat to very moderate, 160°C, 325°F, Gas Mark 3. Serve hot or cold.

For a picnic carry in the tin or bake in a foil dish.

To bake 'blind' put a thick layer of foil into the uncooked pastry shape. This prevents the bottom of the pastry rising. Instead of foil you can use greased greaseproof paper (greasy side next to pastry); top with crusts of bread, dried beans or macaroni. Remove after 15 minutes baking. Cook as the particular recipe.

Galantine of Beef

Derind the bacon rashers, chop and put through a mincer with the meat. The bacon and meat can be chopped in a food processor if more convenient. Blend together the beef, bacon and other ingredients. Grease a 1kg (2¼lb) loaf tin and put in the mixture. Cover with greased foil and stand the tin in a bain-marie (dish of cold water). Bake for 1¾-2 hours in the centre of a slow oven, 150°C, 300°F, Gas Mark 2. To make this galantine easier to slice, put a light weight on top of the mixture as it cools.

If carrying for a picnic, keep in the tin.

Potato Salad

Cook the potatoes in salted water. These can be peeled or skinned after cooking; this is a good idea for it makes sure they do not become over-soft. Dice the potatoes and make the salad while the potatoes are still hot. The golden rule for a perfect potato salad is 'Make when hot, eat when cold'. Blend the salad oil, vinegar, mayonnaise, half the parsley and half the chives. Blend with the potatoes. Garnish with the remaining herbs.

If carrying on a picnic, put into a polythene box.

Mixed Salad

Prepare the ingredients, cut neatly in a uniform size. Always consider the dish with which the salad is to be served. The Galantine of Beef blends with a salad containing a variety of crisp ingredients.

Carry as suggested under Potato Salad, above.

Lemon Sponge

Line two 18-20cm (7-8in) sandwich tins with rounds of greased grease-proof paper; grease and flour the inner sides of the tins. If the tins are well seasoned or a non-stick type, then simply grease and flour the inside of the tins. Make the light whisked sponge and divide the mixture between the tins. Bake for approximately 12 minutes just above the centre of a moderate oven, 180-190°C, 350-375°F, Gas Mark 4-5. Test by pressing gently but firmly on top of the sponge; if no impression is left, the sponge is cooked. Allow to cool for 2-3 minutes in the tins, then turn on to a wire cooling tray. When cold, sandwich together with the ingredients suggested. Top with sugar.

Carry in a polythene box.

Iced Coffee

Freeze the coffee as ice cubes. *Crush* and carry in a vacuum flask (never carry whole ice cubes in a vacuum flask unless approved by the manufacturer). Put very cold milk into a separate vacuum flask.

To Make Sunday Easier

1 Bake the flan one or two days ahead if this is not being frozen; keep in a covered container in the refrigerator.
2 Bake the Galantine of Beef on Saturday. Make the Potato Salad; this improves with being kept for a few days in the refrigerator. Prepare the Mixed Salad ingredients; keep in the salad container in the refrigerator.
3 Bake the sponge cake; this can be filled with the lemon curd and cream and stored in a covered container in the refrigerator.
4 Make and chill the strong coffee if this cannot be frozen as in recipe.

Foods Required

0.75kg (1½lb) topside or chuck steak, 225g (8oz) pork sausage-meat, 85g (3oz) butter, 100g (4oz) Gruyère cheese, 100g (4oz) cream cheese, 150ml (¼pt) double cream or 175g (6oz) cottage cheese for sponge filling, 2tbspn single cream, or milk plus milk for Iced Coffee, 8 eggs, 4 rashers streaky bacon, 175g (6oz) plain flour, 75g (3oz) plain or self-raising flour, 175g (6oz) caster sugar, coffee, 100-175g (4-6oz) lemon curd, 4tbspn mayonnaise (see Menu 34), 1tbspn salad oil, 1tbspn white wine or malt vinegar, ingredients for Mixed Salad (see recipe), 450g (1lb) old or new potatoes, parsley, basil, chives, sage, fresh fruit.

Mixed Salad

Ingredients can include cooked or raw root vegetables such as cooked beetroot, carrots, cucumber and/or chicory, lettuce of various kinds and/or endive or shredded green vegetables, mustard and cress, spring or other onions, radishes, red and green peppers, tomatoes, watercress, hard-boiled eggs.

Do not neglect fruits such as apples, bananas, berry fruits, citrus fruit segments, dried fruits, ripe peaches, pineapples, and various nuts.

Lemon Sponge

Use the ingredients for the very light sponge under Swiss Raspberry Alaska in Menu 30; add 1tspn grated lemon rind to the egg yolks.

For the filling and topping
lemon curd and/or sweetened
  cream or sieved cottage
  cheese
little caster sugar

Iced Coffee

coffee of double strength
cold milk

To Freeze Ahead

Genoese Flan freezes extremely well; defrost slowly at room temperature or carefully reheat in the oven or microwave cooker.
Galantine of Beef also freezes very well; if hastening defrosting, stand the tin in a bain-marie, as when originally baking to avoid drying the beef mixture.
Lemon Sponge: open-freeze, wrap.
Iced Coffee: freeze strong coffee as in recipe.

Chicken Liver Pâté
1 medium onion
225g (8oz) chickens' livers
100g (4oz) butter
salt and pepper
1tspn chopped parsley
2tspn chopped chives
½tspn chopped thyme
2tbspn beef stock or dry sherry
3tbspn double cream

Variations
1 Rub the cooked onion and livers through a sieve.
2 Use calves' liver in place of chickens' liver.

Trout with Almonds
4 fresh trout
salt and pepper
75g (3oz) butter
50g (2oz) blanched almonds

To garnish
lemon wedges

Tomato and Green Pepper Salad
4 medium tomatoes
1 green pepper
2tbspn French Dressing (see Menu 34)
1tbspn chopped chives

Gooseberry Snow
550g (1¼lb) gooseberries
2–3tbspn water
75g (3oz) sugar
3 egg whites
little whipped cream (optional)

To Freeze Ahead
Chicken Liver Pâté for 2–3 weeks only.
Potato Croquettes: either cook and freeze ready for reheating or simply shape mixture, coat and freeze.
Gooseberry Snow: freeze the smooth gooseberry purée, defrost and complete dessert.

Menu 27	Chicken Liver Pâté
Serves 4	Trout with Almonds and Potato Croquettes Green Salad – Tomato and Green Pepper Salad
	Gooseberry Snow

Chicken Liver Pâté
Peel and finely chop the onion; cut the livers into small pieces. Heat half the butter in a large frying pan and fry the onion for 2-3 minutes; take care it does not discolour. Add the livers, salt, pepper and herbs, cook for 3 minutes; stir well during this time so the livers do not dry. Remove from the pan. Put into a food processor or liquidiser. Add the remaining butter, stock or sherry and cream to pan, heat for 1 minute, or until butter melts, stirring well to absorb any remaining meat juices. Add to the livers and onion. Switch on until very smooth. Allow to cool.

Trout with Almonds
Clean the fish, remove the bones; the heads can be cut off if wished. Dry the fish and season. Heat the butter in a frying pan, fry the nuts until golden, remove, then fry the fish until tender. Return the almonds to the pan and heat again for 1 minute. Spoon the butter and nuts over the fish when serving. Garnish with the lemon. (For Potato Croquettes see Menus 50 and 30 (under Fried Potatoes), and Menu 37 for Green Salad.)

Tomato and Green Pepper Salad
Skin and slice the tomatoes; thinly slice the pepper, discard the core and seeds. Put the ingredients on a dish, top with dressing and chives.

Gooseberry Snow
Top and tail the fruit, cook with the water and sugar until soft. Rub through a sieve or liquidise until smooth; allow to cool. Whisk the egg whites until very stiff; fold into the purée. Spoon into glasses and chill well. Top the dessert with whipped cream.

To Make Sunday Easier
1 Pâté can be made several days ahead if covered with melted butter.
2 Clean the fish ready for cooking; make Potato Croquettes.
3 Prepare salad ingredients; put in salad container in refrigerator.
4 Prepare gooseberry purée for dessert.

Foods Required
225g (8oz) chickens' livers, 4 fresh (not smoked) trout, 175g (7oz) butter, approximately 150ml (¼pt) double cream, whipped cream (optional), 3 eggs (whites only used), 75g (3oz) sugar, 2tbspn dry sherry (unless using stock), oil and vinegar or lemon juice for French Dressing (see Menu 34), 50g (2oz) blanched almonds, ingredients for Green Salad and Potato Croquettes (see Menus 37 and 50), 1 medium onion, 4 medium tomatoes, 1 green pepper, chives, parsley, thyme, 1-2 lemons, 550g (1¼lb) gooseberries.

Menu 27
Trout with Almonds and Potato Croquettes, Green Salad, Tomato and Green Pepper Salad

Iced Cucumber Soup

1 onion
1 medium cucumber
25g (1oz) butter
600ml (1pt) chicken stock
salt and pepper
4tbspn double cream

To garnish
lemon wedges

Harvest Chicken

4 large chicken breasts
salt and pepper
1 onion
100g (4oz) mushrooms
25g (1oz) butter or margarine
40g (1½oz) soft breadcrumbs
2tbspn chopped parsley
1 egg yolk

To coat
1 egg
25g (1oz) flour
50g (2oz) soft breadcrumbs

For frying
oil

Potatoes Anna

450g (1lb) potatoes
50g (2oz) butter or fat
salt and pepper

Menu 28	Iced Cucumber Soup
Serves 4	Harvest Chicken
	Potatoes Anna
	Peas à la Française
	Ratatouille
	Strawberry Shortcake

Iced Cucumber Soup

Peel and chop the onion. Peel three-quarters of the cucumber, but leave the peel on the remaining part unless it is very tough for this gives both colour and flavour; chop the cucumber. Heat the butter in a saucepan and fry the vegetables for only 5 minutes; do not allow them to discolour. Add the chicken stock, salt and pepper to taste; simmer for about 25 minutes. Sieve or put into a liquidiser or food processor to give a smooth purée; blend with the cream. Check the seasoning. Put into the freezer or freezing compartment of the refrigerator and leave until lightly iced. Spoon into soup cups and garnish with the lemon.

Harvest Chicken

Carefully cut away the bone from the chicken breasts, put the bones into a saucepan with cold water to cover, add a little salt and pepper and simmer for approximately 1 hour. Do not use giblets in this stock as it needs to be pale for the cucumber soup. Peel and chop the onion, wipe and chop the mushrooms. Heat the butter or margarine in a pan and fry the onion and mushrooms until soft. Add the breadcrumbs, parsley, egg yolk and salt and pepper. Make a cut in each breast portion and insert the stuffing; secure with cocktail sticks. Beat the egg. Season the flour. Coat the chicken with the flour, then the egg and soft breadcrumbs. Heat the oil in a pan and fry the chicken until crisp and brown; remove cocktail sticks.

There are two ways to complete the cooking. You can either lower the heat and continue frying until tender, or transfer the chicken portions to an oven-proof dish and cook for 30 minutes in the hottest part of a moderate oven, 180-190°C, 350-375°F, Gas Mark 4-5.

Potatoes Anna

Peel the potatoes and slice very thinly. Melt the butter or fat. Grease an oven-proof dish or cake tin with some of this. Arrange the potatoes in neat layers with salt and pepper to taste. Brush each layer with the melted butter or fat. Allow about 1¼-1½ hours in the centre of a moderate oven. Although traditionally Potatoes Anna are turned out like a cake and cut in slices, they look as attractive if served in the oven-proof dish garnished with parsley.

Peas à la Française

Wash the lettuce leaves, but do not drain them. Place half the damp leaves in the bottom of a casserole. Add the peas, butter, salt and pepper. Peel the spring onions or peel and slice the onion and place on top of the peas; finally, add the remaining damp lettuce leaves. Cover the casserole tightly. Cook for 35-40 minutes in the coolest part of a moderate oven.

Ratatouille

Peel and chop the onions; peel and crush the garlic; skin and chop the tomatoes. Wash the pepper and cut into slices, discard the core and seeds. Wash, dry and neatly slice or dice the courgettes and aubergine; keep a uniform thickness. Heat the oil, add the onions and garlic, then the tomatoes. Cook slowly until the juice just flows. Add the pepper, courgettes and aubergine, with salt and pepper to taste, and herbs. Cover the pan, simmer gently for about 45 minutes or until all the vegetables are soft but unbroken. Remove the bunch of herbs. Top with chopped parsley.

Strawberry Shortcake

This particular shortcake is more crisp than a sponge and more soft than a very hard shortcake and blends extremely well with soft fruit.

Cream together the butter or margarine and sugar, gradually beat in the eggs. Sieve the flour, or flour and baking powder, with the cornflour, stir into the creamed mixture. Grease and flour two 15-18cm (6-7in) sandwich tins. Divide the mixture between these and press with damp hands until an even layer in each tin. Bake in the centre of a moderate oven, 180°C, 350°F, Gas Mark 4, for approximately 18 minutes until pale golden in colour. Cool for a short time in the tins for shortcakes are rather brittle when warm. Turn out on to a wire cooling tray.

Whip the cream, slice half the strawberries. Spread about half the cream on one layer of shortcake, add the sliced strawberries; sweeten if desired. Put the second layer of shortcake over the fruit and cream. Decorate with whipped cream and the remainder of the strawberries; dust with a little sugar.

To Make Sunday Easier

1 Make and freeze the soup earlier in the week.
2 If you do not freeze the chicken, stuff the portions on Saturday and chill in the refrigerator.
3 Cook Ratatouille ahead; put into an oven-proof dish in the refrigerator ready for reheating.
4 Bake shortcake rounds; store in airtight tin for several days. Fill and top just before lunch.

Foods Required

4 large chicken breasts, 250g (9oz) butter, bottle oil (frying plus 2tbspn), 300ml (½pt) double cream, 4 eggs, 200g (7oz) self-raising flour or plain flour and 1½tspn baking powder, 25g (1oz) cornflour, bread to give 90g (3½oz) soft breadcrumbs, 150g (5oz) caster sugar, 1 large aubergine, 3 medium courgettes, 1 medium cucumber, 1-2 garlic cloves, lettuce, 100g (4oz) mushrooms, 2 small onions, 2 medium onions, small bunch spring onions, 675g (1½lb) fresh peas or 450g (1lb) frozen peas, 450g (1lb) potatoes, 1 red pepper, 350g (12oz) tomatoes, fresh herbs, parsley, 1 lemon, 450-550g (1-1¼lb) small strawberries.

Peas à la Française

outer leaves from 1 lettuce
450g (1lb) shelled fresh or
  frozen peas
25g (1oz) butter
salt and pepper
6 spring onions or 1 onion

Ratatouille

2 small onions
1-2 garlic cloves
350g (12oz) tomatoes
1 red pepper
3 medium courgettes
1 large aubergine
2tbspn oil
salt and pepper
bunch fresh herbs

To garnish
chopped parsley

Strawberry Shortcake

100g (4oz) butter or margarine
100g (4oz) caster sugar
2 eggs
175g (6oz) self-raising flour
  or plain flour and 1½tspn
  baking powder
25g (1oz) cornflour

For the filling
300ml (½pt) double cream*
450-550g (1-1¼lb) small
  strawberries
little caster sugar

*Take out 4tbspn for soup.

To Freeze Ahead

Cucumber soup, remove before meal.
Chicken portions stuffed and coated; open-freeze before packing.
Ratatouille.
Shortcake rounds without filling.

This particular menu based upon veal has other very definite flavours, so choose a wine with a definite flavour. Italian Sauvignon would be a good choice.

Globe Artichokes Vinaigrette

4-6 medium globe artichokes
salt
Vinaigrette Dressing (see Menu 34)

Roast Veal with Forcemeat Balls and Mushroom Purée

1.3-1.5kg (3-3½lb) boned loin veal plus the bones
100g (4oz) butter
2 medium onions
175g (6oz) mushrooms
salt and pepper

Bouillon Potatoes

675g (1½lb) old potatoes
2 medium onions
salt and pepper
300ml (½pt) veal stock
25g (1oz) butter

Broccoli

450-675g (1-1½lb) broccoli
salt
25g (1oz) butter

Mocha Mousse

225g (8oz) plain chocolate
1tbspn water or brandy
2tspn instant coffee powder
3 large eggs
50g (2oz) caster sugar
150ml (¼pt) whipping cream

To Freeze Ahead

Globe artichokes can be frozen; blanch, then pack.
Forcemeat Balls and Mushroom Purée can be frozen.
Mocha Mousse: although this can be frozen it tends to lose some delicate texture.

Menu 29	Globe Artichokes Vinaigrette
Serves 4-6	Roast Veal with Forcemeat Balls and Mushroom Purée
	Bouillon Potatoes – Broccoli
	Mocha Mousse

Globe Artichokes Vinaigrette

Trim the artichoke stalks. Cook steadily in boiling salted water for 20 minutes or until tender at the base. Cool, pull out the centre choke. Serve with the dressing.

Roast Veal with Forcemeat Balls and Mushroom Purée

Cover bones with water, simmer for stock for gravy, mushroom purée and potato dish. Top veal with half the butter, cover with foil or put into a roaster bag. Roast as lower temperature (see page 10). Serve with thickened gravy (see also page 10) and Forcemeat Balls (see Menu 5).

Peel and finely chop the onions, wipe and slice the mushrooms. Heat the butter, cook the onions until nearly tender, add the mushrooms, salt and pepper and simmer for 10 minutes.

Bouillon Potatoes

Peel and thinly slice the potatoes and onions, put in layers in an oven-proof dish, add the seasoned stock. Top with the butter; do not cover the dish. Cook for 1 hour in the centre of a moderate oven.

Cook broccoli as in Menu 47; top with butter.

Mocha Mousse

Break the chocolate into pieces. Place in a good-sized basin with the water or brandy and coffee powder. Melt over a pan of hot water. Separate the eggs, add the yolks and sugar to the basin. Whip until fluffy, remove from the heat, whip until cold. Whisk the cream and the egg whites separately; fold the cream, then the egg whites into the chocolate mixture. Spoon into glasses and chill.

To Make Sunday Easier

1 Cook the artichokes, cover so they do not dry; make the dressings.
2 Prepare the Mushroom Purée; reheat on Sunday. Simmer bones for stock. Make and cook the Forcemeat Balls. Reheat later.
3 Make the Mocha Mousse; cover the glasses with clingfilm.

Foods Required

1.3-1.5kg (3-3½lb) boned loin veal (with bones), 150g (6oz) butter, 50g (2oz) shredded suet, 150ml (¼pt) whipping cream, 4 eggs, flour for gravy, bread to give 100g (4oz) breadcrumbs, oil and vinegar for Vinaigrette Dressing (see Menu 34), 225g (8oz) plain chocolate, 2tspn instant coffee powder, brandy (optional), 50g (2oz) caster sugar, 675g (1½lb) old potatoes, 4 medium onions, 450-675g (1-1½lb) broccoli, 175g (6oz) mushrooms, 4-6 globe artichokes, parsley, 1 lemon.

Menu 28

Iced Cucumber Soup; Harvest Chicken, Potatoes Anna, Peas à la Française, Ratatouille; Strawberry Shortcake

Serve a dry sherry with the flan and a really good red wine (claret) such as a St Emilion from Bordeaux or a Châteauneuf du Pape from the Rhône area.

French Onion Flan

shortcrust pastry made with
    175g (6oz) plain flour, 85g
    (3oz) butter, etc (see Menu
    26)
450g (1lb) onions
50g (2oz) butter or margarine
1tbspn chopped parsley
½-1tspn chopped tarragon
½-1tspn chopped chives
100g (4oz) Gruyère cheese
3 egg yolks*
150ml (¼pt) milk or single
    cream
salt and pepper

*Use egg whites in dessert.

Variations
1 Use 2 eggs in place of egg
yolks.
2 Spinach Flan: use same
weight of cooked finely
chopped spinach.

Grilled Steaks with Maître d'hôtel Butter

For the Maître d'hôtel Butter
50g (2oz) butter
1-2tbspn chopped parsley
salt and pepper
little lemon juice

40-50g (1½-2oz) butter
4 fillet or rump steaks 2cm
    (¾in) in thickness
4 large tomatoes
small parsley sprigs

Fried Potatoes

450g (1lb) potatoes
oil or fat

Variation
Parisienne Potatoes: make small
balls of the raw potatoes with a
vegetable scoop; fry as the
method given.

When deep-frying, never overfill pan with oil or fat or food.

Menu 30	French Onion Flan
Serves 4	Grilled Steaks with Maître d'hôtel Butter and Grilled Tomatoes
	Fried Potatoes — Carrots Vichy — Peas
	Swiss Raspberry Alaska

French Onion Flan

Roll out the pastry, line a 20cm (8in) flan dish, tin or flan ring on an upturned baking tray. Bake 'blind' as described in Menu 26 for only 15 minutes. Meanwhile, peel and very thinly slice the onions; heat the butter or margarine in a frying pan, add the onions together with the chopped herbs and fry gently until tender. Do not allow to brown. Spoon the onions into the partially cooked pastry case. Grate the cheese very finely. Beat the egg yolks with the milk or cream, add the cheese, salt and pepper to taste. Pour over the onions. Return the flan to the oven, lower the heat to slow, 150°C, 300°F, Gas Mark 2, and bake for a further 30 minutes until the filling and pastry are firm. Serve hot or cold.

Grilled Steaks with Maître d'hôtel Butter

Cream the 50g (2oz) butter with the parsley, salt, pepper and lemon juice. Divide into 4 pats; chill until hard. Melt the second amount of butter, brush half over the steaks, put on to the grill pan. Pre-heat the grill on high. Cook as follows: rare (under-done), 2-3 minutes on either side; medium cooked, as rare, plus 4-5 minutes on lower heat; well done, as rare, plus 6-7 minutes on lower heat. After turning the steaks, brush with the remaining butter before continuing to cook. Halve and season the tomatoes, add to the grill during the cooking period. Top the steaks with the Maître d'hôtel Butter; arrange the tomatoes and parsley around the meat.

Fried Potatoes

Peel the potatoes; cut into chips or slices. Keep in cold water until just before cooking; dry on absorbent paper or a cloth. Good fried potatoes need a pan of deep oil or fat; modern electric fryers are excellent. The best results are obtained by frying twice; the first time to cook the potatoes, the second time to crisp and brown them. Heat the oil or fat with the frying basket to 170°C, 345°F, or until a cube of day-old bread turns golden in 30-45 seconds. Put some potatoes into the pan. Cook steadily until tender; timing will depend upon the thickness, but will be about 4-6 minutes. Remove the potatoes, fry a second batch if required. This stage can be done earlier in the day. Just before the meal reheat the oil or fat, this time to 190°C, 375°F. Put in the potatoes and fry for 1-2 minutes until brown and crisp. Drain on absorbent paper.

Potatoes can be fried in shallow fat, but this means turning them over several times in the hot fat.

Potato Croquettes as given in Menu 50 should be deep-fried at approximately 185°C, 365°F, for 3-4 minutes or until brown, or carefully fried in shallow fat.

Carrots Vichy

Peel and slice the carrots. Heat the butter in a saucepan, add the carrots, turn in the butter; add the stock, salt and pepper to taste. Bring the liquid to the boil, cook steadily for 15-20 minutes. Remove the lid after 5 minutes so the liquid gradually evaporates. The carrots should not require straining. Top with parsley. Method for cooking Peas, see Menu 43.

Swiss Raspberry Alaska

Line a large Swiss roll tin measuring approximately 23 × 32cm (9 × 13in) with greased greaseproof paper.

*The whisked eggs and sugar aerate this sponge, so plain flour, without any raising agent, can be used. If, however, you are new to cooking, you may feel happier using self-raising flour or adding ½tspn baking powder to plain flour.

Put the eggs and sugar into a large mixing bowl. Whisk until thick and creamy. This can be done with an electric whisk. The mixture should be sufficiently thick to see the trail of the whisk. Sift the flour and fold into the mixture with a metal spoon. Pour into the tin. Bake for 9-10 minutes towards the top of a moderately hot oven, 190°C, 375°F, Gas Mark 5, until firm to the touch. Turn out on to sugared paper. Cover with a piece of greaseproof paper. Roll and allow to cool.

Have ready the ice-cream—it should be soft enough to spread. Mash most of the raspberries with a little sugar. Unroll the sponge and spread with the mashed raspberries; top with the ice-cream and reroll. If you can freeze the dessert for a very short time at this stage it is a good idea, for it makes quite certain that the ice-cream is sufficiently cold to withstand the subsequent heat of the oven. Place on an oven-proof serving dish. Make sure the oven is pre-heated to very hot, 230-240°C, 450-475°F, Gas Mark 8-9. Whisk the egg whites until very stiff; fold in the sugar. Spoon or pipe over the Swiss roll, making quite sure the entire cake is covered. Put into the oven and bake for 3 minutes or until a golden colour. Top with the remaining raspberries and serve.

To Make Sunday Easier

1 Cook the flan on Saturday unless it is being frozen.
2 Prepare and chill the Maître d'hôtel Butter.
3 Make the Swiss roll; unroll and fill before coating with meringue.

Foods Required

4 fillet or rump steaks, 300g (10oz) butter, 150ml (¼pt) milk or single cream, 6 or 7 eggs, 100g (4oz) Gruyère cheese, ingredients for ice-cream (see Menu 18) or block ice-cream, 175g (6oz) plain flour, 75g (3oz) self-raising flour, 250g (9oz) caster sugar, oil or fat for frying, 4 large tomatoes, 675-900g (1½-2lb) fresh peas, 450g (1lb) onions, 450g (1lb) potatoes, 450g (1lb) carrots, parsley, tarragon, chives, 1 lemon, 350-450g (¾-1lb) raspberries.

Carrots Vichy

450g (1lb) carrots
25g (1oz) butter
300ml (½pt) chicken stock
salt and pepper

To garnish
1-2tbspn chopped parsley

Swiss Raspberry Alaska

For the sponge
3 large eggs
100g (4oz) caster sugar
75g (3oz) flour*

little caster sugar (see method)
ice-cream (see Menu 18) or a
    family-size brick of ice-cream
350-450g (¾-1lb) raspberries

For the meringue
3-4 egg whites
75-100g (3-4oz) caster sugar

Variations
1 Use other fruit instead of raspberries.
2 Serve with Melba Sauce (see Menu 31).

To Freeze Ahead

French Onion Flan: best if cream used in filling.
Swiss roll: filled or plain. If filled it must be defrosted until the sponge softens before coating with meringue; take care the ice-cream does not become too soft.

Although serving meat as a main course, a well-chilled rosé wine would be a good choice or have a good dry cider and fruit juice for the children.

Asparagus Creams
350g (12oz) fresh cooked or canned asparagus
150ml (¼pt) asparagus stock from can or cooking
15g (½oz) gelatine
200ml (7½fl oz) whipping cream
salt and pepper
squeeze lemon juice

To garnish
50g (2oz) peeled prawns or smoked salmon

Variation
Serve in ramekin dishes, top with the garnish.

Cold Meat Platter
Allow 100-175g (4-6oz) cold meat per person; choose a selection of kinds of salami, tongue, ham, etc.

Fresh Peach Melba

For the Melba Sauce
1tspn arrowroot
5tbspn water
225g (8oz) fresh or frozen raspberries
25g (1oz) caster sugar
3tbspn redcurrant jelly

4-6 medium fresh ripe peaches
block vanilla ice-cream or ice-cream made as in Menu 18

To Freeze Ahead
Asparagus Creams: allow to set, then freeze.
Melba Sauce and ice-cream can be frozen: it is sensible to have supplies of both these items.

Menu 31	Asparagus Creams
Serves 4-6	Cold Meat Platter with Potato and Mixed Salads
	Fresh Peach Melba

Asparagus Creams
Cut the asparagus into small pieces. Save 4 or 6 good-shaped tips. Rub the remaining spears through a sieve or put into a food processor or liquidiser to make a smooth purée. Heat the asparagus liquid, add the gelatine, stir until dissolved. Blend with the asparagus purée. Chill until beginning to set. Whip the cream until it stands in soft peaks (whipping cream gives a more delicate flavour than double cream). Fold into the jellied asparagus, add salt, pepper and lemon juice. Spoon into 4-6 oiled individual moulds. Allow to set. Turn out and top with the asparagus tips and a few prawns or small pieces of smoked salmon. Serve with brown bread and butter.

Cold Meat Platter
Arrange the meats on a flat platter so everyone can see the selection available. Garnish with some of the salad ingredients. Recipes for Potato Salad and Mixed Salad are given in Menu 26.

Fresh Peach Melba
Blend the arrowroot and water, put into the saucepan with the raspberries, sugar and jelly. Stir over a low heat until clear and thickened. Sieve if desired; allow to cool. Skin the peaches by putting them in very hot water for a few seconds, then removing the skins. Put the ice-cream into 4 or 6 glasses, top with halved peaches and the sauce.

To Make Sunday Easier
1   Make the Asparagus Creams on Saturday if not freezing these.
2   Prepare salad ingredients and any dressings required.
3   Make the Melba Sauce. Make and freeze the ice-cream.

Foods Required
Selection of cold meats, 50g (2oz) peeled prawns or smoked salmon, brown bread and butter, 200ml (7½fl oz) whipping cream, block ice-cream or ingredients for ice-cream (see Menu 18), 15g (½oz) gelatine, 25g (1oz) caster sugar, 1tspn arrowroot, 3tbspn redcurrant jelly, 350g (12oz) fresh or canned asparagus, ingredients for Potato and Mixed Salads and dressings (see Menu 26), 225g (8oz) fresh or frozen raspberries, 4-6 medium fresh peaches, 1 lemon.

Menu 30
Swiss Raspberry Alaska

Menu 32

Serves 6

Seafood Quiche

Chicken à la King with Rice
Cauliflower Polonaise — Vichy Courgettes

Brandied Fruit Mousse

Seafood Quiche

shortcrust pastry made with
   175g (6oz) plain flour, etc
   (see Menu 26)
1 small crab or 100g (4oz)
   defrosted frozen crab meat
100g (4oz) smoked mackerel
50g (2oz) peeled prawns
2 egg yolks*
1 egg
150ml (¼pt) single cream or
   milk
salt and pepper
few drops Tabasco sauce
1tspn grated lemon rind

To garnish
lemon and cucumber slices

*Save whites for meringues or freeze (see Menus 23 and 24).

Seafood Quiche

Roll out the pastry and line a 23cm (9in) flan dish; bake 'blind' as described in Menu 26 for 15 minutes in a moderately hot oven, 200°C, 400°F, Gas Mark 6, or until just golden and firm in texture. If using fresh crab, remove the flesh from the body and claws, retain the small claws to garnish the dish. Flake the mackerel. Mix the various fish together, place evenly in the pastry case. Beat the egg yolks and egg with the cream or milk and remaining ingredients. Pour over the fish. Return to the centre of the oven, lowering the heat to cool, 150°C, 300°F, Gas Mark 2, for 45 minutes, or until set. Garnish with lemon and cucumber slices and the crab claws. Serve hot or cold.

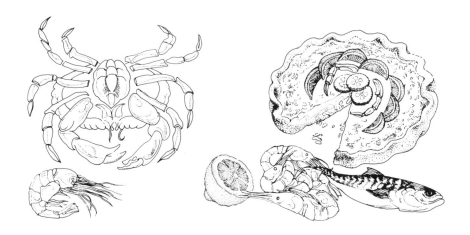

Chicken à la King

chicken about 1.35kg (3lb) in
   weight
salt and pepper
450ml (¾pt) chicken stock
2 medium onions
100g (4oz) very small button
   mushrooms
75g (3oz) butter or chicken fat
50g (2oz) flour
300ml (½pt) milk
175g (6oz) canned sweetcorn
2-3tbspn chopped parsley
4tbspn chopped fresh or
   canned red peppers

Variation
Use a ready-cooked chicken; remove bones, simmer these for stock or use stock cubes.

Chicken à la King

Cook the chicken by simmering in well-seasoned water to cover. Allow 15 minutes per 450g (1lb) and 15 minutes over, but do not over-cook since the flesh is reheated in the sauce. When cooked, lift from the liquid, cut all the meat from the bones. Return the bones to the stock and boil steadily until reduced to 600ml (1pt). Strain carefully, measure out 450ml (¾pt) for this dish, save remainder for cooking courgettes. Peel and chop the onions; wipe the mushrooms. Heat the butter or chicken fat in a saucepan, stir in the onions and cook gently until nearly tender. Add the mushrooms and continue cooking for 3-4 minutes. Stir in the flour, then add the chicken stock and milk. Bring the sauce to the boil and stir over a low heat until slightly thickened; at this stage the sauce should not be too thick. Dice the chicken neatly, add to the sauce with the sweetcorn, half the parsley, salt and pepper to taste. Heat gently for 6-7 minutes, stir once or twice. Garnish with the rest of the parsley and the chopped red pepper.

Rice

There are many ways of cooking rice, but this is a very simple method. Put the rice, cold water and salt into a pan. Bring the water to the boil, stir briskly with a fork. Cover the pan and lower the heat. Simmer gently for 15 minutes; at the end of this time the liquid should have evaporated and all the rice grains should be cooked and separate. If any liquid remains, just uncover the pan and cook gently for 2-3 minutes. These proportions use twice as much water as rice. If using par-boiled rice, use 2½ times the water and simmer for 20 minutes.

Cauliflower Polonaise

Prepare the cauliflower. For a buffet meal divide into very small florets and cook only for a short time. Top with the crumbs and other ingredients.

Vichy Courgettes

Wash and dry the courgettes. Remove the tough ends, then slice thinly; do not peel. Heat the butter in a pan, toss the sliced courgettes in this, add the stock, with a little salt and pepper. Cover the pan, simmer steadily for 10 minutes, or until tender. If any liquid remains, lift the lid towards the end of the cooking time. There should be no need to strain this vegetable. Top with parsley.

Brandied Fruit Mousse

Sprinkle the gelatine on the brandy. Dissolve over very hot water. Stir to blend. Separate the egg yolks from the whites. Blend the yolks with 25g (1oz) of the sugar and the milk. Cook over a pan of very hot, but not boiling, water until a thick coating custard; stir from time to time. Add the dissolved gelatine. Allow the mixture to cool and begin to stiffen. Whisk the egg whites until very stiff, fold in 25g (1oz) sugar. Whip the cream, fold into the custard mixture together with the egg whites. Put most of the raspberries and strawberries into 6 glasses; sprinkle with the remaining sugar. Top with the brandy mousse. Chill well, then decorate with the remaining fruit.

To Make Sunday Easier

1 Bake quiche if not freezing this; garnish on Sunday.
2 Cook Chicken à la King; cover tightly and reheat in low oven.
3 Prepare topping for cauliflower; cover tightly, put in oven-proof dish. Reheat for short time on Sunday.
4 Make Brandied Fruit Mousse.

Foods Required

1.35kg (3lb) chicken, small fresh or 100g (4oz) frozen crab, 100g (4oz) smoked mackerel, 50g (2oz) peeled prawns, 200g (8oz) butter, 150ml (¼pt) double cream, 150ml (¼pt) single cream, 8 eggs (6 whites only used), 600ml (1pt) milk, 225g (8oz) flour, 75g (3oz) caster sugar, 225g (8oz) long grain rice, Tabasco sauce, 3tbspn brandy, 1tspn gelatine, 175g (6oz) canned sweetcorn, 450-675g (1-1½lb) courgettes, 100g (4oz) small button mushrooms, 2 medium onions, 4tbspn red peppers, piece cucumber, 1 large cauliflower, parsley, 225g (8oz) raspberries, 225g (8oz) strawberries, 1 lemon.

Rice

225g (8oz) long grain rice
just over 450ml (¾pt or 16fl oz) water
½-1 tspn salt, depending upon personal taste

Cauliflower Polonaise

See Menu 10; use a good-sized cauliflower.

Vichy Courgettes

450-675g (1-1½lb) courgettes
25g (1oz) butter
150ml (¼pt) chicken stock
salt and pepper

To garnish
chopped parsley

Brandied Fruit Mousse

1tspn gelatine
3tbspn brandy
3 eggs
75g (3oz) caster sugar
300ml (½pt) milk
150ml (¼pt) double cream
225g (8oz) raspberries
225g (8oz) strawberries

Variations
1 Use cherry brandy in the mousse and dessert cherries instead of berry fruits.
2 Use cassis in the mousse and lightly-cooked blackcurrants instead of berry fruits.
3 Use orange juice in place of brandy.

To Freeze Ahead

Seafood Quiche freezes particularly well if cream used in filling. If serving hot, take care not to over-cook when reheating.
Chicken à la King: do not over-cook chicken if freezing; reheat gently over hot water or in a microwave cooker.
Rice: cook and par-freeze, then separate grains with fork. To reheat, tip into pan of cold water, bring to boil slowly, then strain.

This informal meal is ideal for carrying into the garden or having on a tray. It makes a Ploughman's Lunch considerably more interesting. Offer chilled beer, white or rosé wines.

Speedy Liver Pâté
225g (8oz) lambs' or calves' liver
2 fat bacon rashers
1 medium onion
1 garlic clove
100g (4oz) butter
4-5tbspn single cream
2tbspn chopped parsley
salt and pepper

Cheeses
See selection in Menu 41.

Cherry Sponge Flan

For the sponge
2 eggs
75g (3oz) caster sugar
50g (2oz) flour

For the filling
50g (2oz) caster sugar
300ml (½pt) water
450-550g (1-1¼lb) dessert cherries
1tspn arrowroot
2tbspn redcurrant jelly

To Freeze Ahead
This particular pâté freezes well for 1-2 weeks.
Cumberland Sauce freezes for up to 6 months.
Sponges freeze perfectly for 3 months; open-freeze, then wrap. A sponge flan can be filled and frozen if preferred.

Menu 33	Speedy Liver Pâté with Cumberland Sauce
Serves 4-5	Selection of Cheeses — lettuce — tomatoes
	Cherry Sponge Flan

Speedy Liver Pâté
Slice the liver thinly, derind and chop the bacon, peel and chop the onion and garlic. Heat the butter in a frying pan, add the bacon and onion, and cook gently for 4-5 minutes; stir well so the foods do not discolour. Add the liver and cook for about 4 minutes; do not over-cook. Remove all the ingredients from the pan, add the cream, heat for 1 minute, stir well to absorb all meat juices. Put all the ingredients with salt and pepper to taste into a liquidiser or food processor. Switch on until as smooth a pâté as desired. Chill and serve with toast or crispbread and butter.

Cumberland Sauce given in Menu 4 is a good accompaniment to this.

Cheeses
Arrange cheeses on a large board with quartered tomatoes, lettuce, pickles and chutney. Cut French bread into thick slices; serve with butter.

Cherry Sponge Flan
Grease and flour a 20-23cm (8-9in) sponge flan tin and pre-heat the oven as directed for Swiss roll in Menu 30. Prepare the sponge as for the Swiss roll, pour into the sponge flan tin and bake for 10-12 minutes until firm. Cool for 2-3 minutes, tap the tin to loosen the sponge, turn out and cool. Meanwhile, heat the sugar and water to make a syrup. Stone the cherries, poach for a few minutes in the syrup. Drain the fruit through a sieve. Boil the syrup until just about 150ml (¼pt). Blend the arrowroot with this syrup, put into the saucepan with the redcurrant jelly, stir over a low heat until thickened and clear. Arrange the cherries in the flan. Brush or spoon over the cool glaze; leave until lightly set. Serve with cream.

To Make Sunday Easier
1 Prepare pâté and Cumberland Sauce (see Menu 4); chill or freeze. Wash lettuce when purchased; crisp in salad container in refrigerator.
2 Make and fill flan.

Foods Required
225g (8oz) lambs' or calves' liver, 100g (4oz) butter, cheeses, 150ml (¼pt) single cream, 2 eggs, 2 fat bacon rashers, 50g (2oz) flour, 150g (5oz) caster sugar, ingredients for Cumberland Sauce (see Menu 4), French bread, bread for toast or crispbread, 1tspn arrowroot, 2tbspn redcurrant jelly, chutney, pickle, 1 medium onion, 1 garlic clove, tomatoes, lettuce, parsley, 450-550g (1-1¼lb) dessert cherries.

Menu 34
Crudités with Mayonnaise and French Dressing; Sandwich Layer Gâteau, Chicken and Mushroom Salad, Pineapple and Apple Coleslaw; Fresh Fruit

Crudités

young carrots, part of a cauliflower, celery heart, piece of cucumber, spring onions, red and green peppers, radishes, firm tomatoes

To serve
mayonnaise
French Dressing

Mayonnaise

2 eggs
up to 300ml (½pt) olive oil or best quality salad oil
½tspn mustard powder or 1tspn French mustard
salt and pepper
1-2tbspn white wine vinegar or lemon juice
1tbspn boiling water (optional)

French Dressing

2-3tspn French mustard or 1tspn made English mustard
salt and pepper
½tspn sugar
150ml (¼pt) olive, corn or salad oil
4-5tbspn lemon juice or red or white wine vinegar
1-2tbspn freshly chopped herbs (including crushed garlic)

Sandwich Layer Gâteau

3-4 eggs
1 green pepper
5tbspn mayonnaise
salt and pepper
2 large tomatoes
225g (8oz) cooked ham
1tspn made mustard
175g (6oz) Cheddar cheese
450g (1lb) cream cheese
2-3tbspn chopped parsley
1 large sandwich loaf
butter (see method)
little milk (see method)

To garnish
black and green olives, gherkins, tomato slices, lettuce

Menu 34	Crudités with Mayonnaise and French Dressing
Serves 6-8	Sandwich Layer Gâteau Chicken and Mushroom Salad Pineapple and Apple Coleslaw
	Fresh Fruit—Cheeses

Crudités

Prepare the vegetables; remember they will be eaten with the fingers, so keep a little of the stalk on the spring onions and radishes. Cut the tomatoes into quarters and other vegetables into neat pieces. Pack in a polythene box, then arrange on a large platter with containers of mayonnaise and French Dressing so each person may dip in.

When serving at home you can put a selection of vegetables on individual plates and give each person a small dish of mayonnaise and one of French Dressing.

Mayonnaise

Make sure the eggs and oil are at the same room temperature before preparing the dressing. Separate the eggs; put the yolks into a clean dry bowl, add the mustard, salt and pepper, and whisk together. Gradually whisk in the oil, drop by drop, until the mixture thickens. You need not use the full amount of oil—this depends upon personal taste—but the more oil you use the thicker the mayonnaise will be. Finally, whisk in the vinegar or lemon juice. If the boiling water is used it should be whisked in at the end.

If making the mayonnaise in a liquidiser or food processor you can make a lighter mayonnaise by using the whole eggs (see Menu 22). *Note* For this particular menu you will need about double the amount of mayonnaise. It is easier to make this in two batches.

French Dressing

Blend the mustard, salt, pepper and sugar with the oil, then add the lemon juice or vinegar (adjust the amount to personal taste and particular foods). When using vinegar the sauce can be termed Vinaigrette. If adding herbs, put these in at the end of the process. You can make a larger amount and keep it in a screw-topped bottle, but if herbs are added the dressing tastes better if freshly made.

Sandwich Layer Gâteau

Hard-boil the eggs; shell and chop. Chop the pepper; discard the core and seeds. Blend the eggs, pepper and 3tbspn mayonnaise together. Season to taste.

Skin and finely chop the tomatoes. Chop the ham, mix with the mustard, chopped tomatoes and a little salt and pepper.

Grate the Cheddar cheese, blend with 50g (2oz) cream cheese, 1tbspn chopped parsley and 1tbspn mayonnaise.

Cut away the crusts from the loaf, then cut lengthways into 4 slices. Spread the first slice with a little butter, add the egg mixture; put on the second slice, butter, add the ham filling, put on the third slice, butter, top with the cheese mixture; put on the final layer of bread.

Blend the remaining cream cheese, mayonnaise and parsley. Add a very little milk to give a soft spreading consistency, season well. Spread over the top and sides of the loaf. Garnish with the olives, gherkins, sliced tomatoes and lettuce.

Put a long strip of double foil into a polythene container. Place the loaf on top of this, then cover the container and chill well. The foil makes it easy to lift the loaf from the container.

Chicken and Mushroom Salad

Mix together the mayonnaise, lemon juice and cream with a litle salt and pepper. Dice the chicken; wipe and slice the mushrooms; dice the pepper, discard the core and seeds. Blend the ingredients together. Allow to stand for 1 hour. Serve on a bed of prepared lettuce; slice the tomatoes and arrange around the edge of the dish.

Pineapple and Apple Coleslaw

Blend the dressing and mayonnaise together. Peel and dice the apples, put into the dressing and mayonnaise to prevent discolouring. Cut the pineapple rings into small pieces, add to the apple mixture. Finely shred the cabbage and blend the ingredients well. Spoon into a container and top with the walnuts.

To Make Sunday Easier

1   Prepare Crudités; keep in salad container in refrigerator. Make mayonnaise and French Dressing: put into container for picnic.
2   Prepare Sandwich Layer Gâteau; store in container in refrigerator; remember to put sharp knife in readiness.
3   Make Chicken and Mushroom Salad—this improves by standing overnight in refrigerator.
4   Pack cheeses for the picnic.
5   Pack plates, paper napkins, cutlery required.

Foods Required

350g (12oz) cooked chicken, 225g (8oz) cooked ham, approximately 75g (3oz) butter, 175g (6oz) Cheddar cheese, 450g (1lb) cream cheese, selection of cheeses (see Menu 41), 2tbspn double cream, 5-6 eggs, little milk, ½tspn sugar, 1 large sandwich loaf, 450ml (¾pt) olive oil or salad oil if making mayonnaise and French Dressing, French mustard, mustard, 1-2tbspn white wine vinegar or lemon juice, black and green olives, gherkins, 2tbspn chopped walnuts, 2 green peppers, 6-7 large tomatoes, lettuce, 100g (4oz) button mushrooms, ½ small white cabbage heart, vegetables for Crudités (see recipe), parsley, fresh herbs including garlic, 2 dessert apples, 4 rings fresh or canned pineapple, lemons to give 1tbspn juice plus 4-5tbspn red or white wine vinegar, fresh fruit.

Chicken and Mushroom Salad

3tbspn mayonnaise
1tbspn lemon juice
2tbspn double cream
salt and pepper
350g (12oz) cooked chicken, preferably breast meat
100g (4oz) button mushrooms
1 small green pepper
1 lettuce
3-4 tomatoes

Pineapple and Apple Coleslaw

5tbspn French Dressing
3tbspn mayonnaise
2 dessert apples
4 rings fresh or canned pineapple
½ small white cabbage heart

To garnish
2tbspn chopped walnuts

To Freeze Ahead

This menu is not suitable for freezing individual dishes, but you could freeze individual foods such as a sliced loaf for the Sandwich Layer Gâteau; grated cheese mixture; cooked chicken for the Chicken Salad.

Using Raw Mushrooms

Raw mushrooms are not used as often as they might be—they are delicious. Choose perfect plump button mushrooms; wipe with kitchen paper or wash in cold water if very dirty and dry well.

Making Coleslaw

Although the Dutch white cabbage is usual for coleslaw you can use any tender cabbage heart, including red cabbage. This is not often used except for pickling, but cook as described in Menu 43, or as in the more interesting recipe in Menu 3.

A well-chilled white wine, such as a Sancerre from the Loire district would be a good choice for this menu. If serving fruit drinks, choose grapefruit juice.

Jellied Consommé
1.2 litre (2pt) consommé (see Menu 21)
15g (½oz) gelatine
1tbspn lemon juice

To garnish
chopped parsley
yoghurt or sour cream
lemon wedges

Veal in Paprika Sauce
4 veal escalopes
salt and pepper
4 rashers lean streaky bacon
50g (2oz) butter
150ml (¼pt) double cream
1tbspn tomato purée
1tspn paprika
4 slices, 100-175g (4-6oz) Gruyère or Cheddar cheese

To garnish
sprigs of parsley
4 lemon slices

Stuffed Peaches
150ml (¼pt) double cream
175g (6oz) raspberries
1 macaroon biscuit
50g (2oz) caster sugar
150ml (¼pt) water
1tbspn lemon juice
4 large ripe peaches

To Freeze Ahead
Consommé freezes well; you may prefer to make fairly large amounts and freeze this in suitable sized containers, then serve hot or cold.

Menu 35
Jellied Consommé

Serves 4

Veal in Paprika Sauce
Creamed Potatoes—Cauliflower

Stuffed Peaches

Jellied Consommé
Make the consommé as the recipe in Menu 21. Dissolve the gelatine in the hot consommé, add the lemon juice. Leave until lightly set, then either whisk with a fork or cut into small pieces and spoon into chilled soup cups. Garnish with chopped parsley and a spoonful of yoghurt or sour cream and serve with thick lemon wedges.

Veal in Paprika Sauce
Beat the slices of veal with a damp rolling pin to make them very thin; season lightly. Derind and halve the bacon rashers. Heat the butter in a large frying pan, cook the escalopes until tender; this takes 8-10 minutes. Blend the cream, tomato purée and paprika; pour into the frying pan. Stir well so the sauce absorbs the meat juices; heat gently, but do not boil. Turn the meat in the sauce to coat both sides; top each piece of veal with a slice of cheese, then 2 halved bacon rashers. Place the frying pan under a pre-heated grill for 2-3 minutes. Garnish with the parsley and lemon slices.

The method for cooking Creamed Potatoes is described in Menu 7 and for Cauliflower in Menu 23.

Stuffed Peaches
Whip the cream, mash the raspberries, chop the macaroon. Mix these ingredients together with half the sugar. Heat the water, lemon juice and remaining sugar. Skin and halve the peaches; poach in the syrup for 2-3 minutes only (this prevents the fruit discolouring), then allow to cool. Drain and fill with the raspberry mixture. The syrup could be frozen very lightly and spooned around the cold peaches, or this can be saved and put into a fruit salad.

To Make Sunday Easier
1 Prepare consommé when convenient; chop parsley, put in plastic bag in refrigerator.
2 Flatten veal ready for cooking; prepare bacon and cheese.
3 Blend ingredients for filling peaches; chill in refrigerator.

Foods Required
4 veal escalopes, beef for consommé (see Menu 21), 75g (3oz) butter, 100-175g (4-6oz) Gruyère or Cheddar cheese, 300ml (½pt) double cream, milk, small carton yoghurt or soured cream, 4 rashers streaky bacon, 50g (2oz) caster sugar, 15g (½oz) gelatine, paprika, 1tbspn tomato purée, 1 macaroon biscuit, 450-675g (1-1½lb) potatoes, 1 cauliflower, parsley, 3-4 lemons, 4 large ripe peaches, 175g (6oz) raspberries.

Menu 36
Barbecued Chicken and Sauce, Jacket Potatoes; Mincemeat Apples

Cheese Dip
225g (8oz) Cheddar, Gouda or
 other hard cheese
2tbspn mayonnaise (see Menu
 34)
6tbspn yoghurt
2tbspn tomato ketchup
salt and pepper

Tuna Dip
200g (7oz) can tuna in oil
2tbspn yoghurt
100g (4oz) cottage cheese
1tbspn lemon juice
2tbspn chopped fennel leaves
 or parsley

Dippers
plain biscuits, potato crisps,
carrots, radishes, spring onions

Barbecued Chicken
50g (2oz) butter
salt and pepper
4 chicken portions

Barbecue Sauce
1 large onion
2 garlic cloves
2tbspn oil
397g (14oz) can plum tomatoes
2tbspn sweet pickle (see
 method)
1tbspn cider vinegar or white
 wine vinegar
1tbspn brown sugar
2tbspn tomato ketchup
2tspn French mustard
1tspn Worcestershire sauce
salt and pepper

Menu 36	Cheese Dip – Tuna Dip
Serves 4	Barbecued Chicken and Sauce
	Jacket Potatoes – Tomato and Pepper Salad
	Mincemeat Apples

Cheese Dip
Grate the cheese and blend with the other ingredients; spoon into a small bowl.

Tuna Dip
Drain, then flake the canned fish; blend with the other ingredients. Put into a small bowl.

Arrange both dips on a tray and put the 'dippers' around.

Barbecued Chicken
If using a barbecue fire in the garden, make sure the coals are glowing red before commencing cooking.

Melt the butter, add a little salt and pepper. Brush the chicken joints with this, place over the hot barbecue and cook for about 15 minutes, or until tender. Turn once or twice, and each time you turn the joints brush them with more butter.

You can, of course, grill the chicken in the usual way and then take it into the garden. A better way of cooking for outdoor eating is to use a microwave cooker. This is portable and can be used in a power plug in, or near, the garden. It cooks the food rapidly, so each dish can be prepared in record time. To cook chicken joints by microwave, put into a ceramic dish, brush with a little butter (you need less fat in this method of cooking), cover with clingfilm. Portions of chicken will take only 8 minutes per 450g (1lb); turn once during cooking, wrap in foil at the end of the time and stand for 5 minutes. Chicken joints can be tenderised in the microwave cooker, then placed over the barbecue fire and basted with the sauce below.

Barbecue Sauce
Peel and finely chop the onion and garlic. Heat the oil in a strong saucepan, add the onion and garlic. Cook over the barbecue fire, or on top of the cooker, until soft; do not allow to brown. Blend in the remaining ingredients, stir briskly to break up the tomatoes and the sweet pickle if this is rather lumpy. Heat over the barbecue or on top of the cooker; keep warm while cooking the other foods.

If using a microwave cooker, put the oil with the chopped onion and garlic into a ceramic mixing bowl or large jug. Cover with clingfilm, cook for 4 minutes or until tender on HIGH. Chop the tomatoes and pickle, then blend these and all the other ingredients with the onions and garlic. Cover the container once again with the clingfilm; cook on HIGH for a further 4 minutes. Allow to stand while cooking the other foods. Microwave-cooked sauces keep hot for a long time, but it is very simple to return the container to the microwave cooker for a minute before serving the meal to ensure that the sauce is very hot.

Jacket Potatoes

Wash, dry and prick the potatoes. Wrap in foil if cooking over the barbecue; allow 1-1¼ hours. Give the same cooking time in a moderate oven, 190°C, 375°F, Gas Mark 5; do not wrap in foil. 4 potatoes take 12-14 minutes on HIGH in a microwave cooker. After cooking, wrap in foil; allow to stand for 5 minutes. Blend the cottage cheese, seasoning and chives. Cut each potato, top with the cheese mixture.

Tomato and Pepper Salad

Quarter the lettuce and tomatoes; cut the peppers into rings, discard the cores and seeds. Serve with the dressing as a 'dip'.

Mincemeat Apples

Core the apples, slit the skin around the centre, fill with the mincemeat. If cooking over the barbecue fire, wrap in foil and allow ¾-1 hour. The apples take the same time in a moderate oven; do not wrap in foil. If using a microwave oven, prick the apple skins, put into a ceramic dish and fill. Cover the dish with clingfilm. Cook for 5-6 minutes on HIGH.

To Make Sunday Easier

Prepare the dips; cover and store in the refrigerator overnight.

Foods Required

4 chicken portions, 50g (2oz) butter, 225g (8oz) cottage cheese, 225g (8oz) Cheddar, Gouda or other hard cheese, 150ml (5fl oz/8tbspn) yoghurt, 1tbspn brown sugar, 2tbspn sweet pickle, plain biscuits, potato crisps, 4tbspn tomato ketchup, 2tbspn oil, 2tbspn mayonnaise (see Menu 34), 1tbspn cider vinegar or white wine vinegar, French mustard, Worcestershire sauce, ingredients for French Dressing (see Menu 34), 4tbspn mincemeat, 200g (7oz) can tuna in oil, 397g (14oz) can plum tomatoes, lettuce, 1 large onion, 2 garlic cloves, 8 medium tomatoes, 1 green pepper, 1 red pepper, 4 medium to large potatoes, carrots, radishes, spring onions, fennel leaves or parsley, chives, 4 cooking apples, 1 lemon.

Perfect Cooking

This depends upon good flavour, so develop a critical palate in order to adjust flavours as you cook. Use foods in season, when they are at their best as well as their cheapest. Learn the right technique of blending ingredients, eg 'folding' is a gentle action, not to be confused with 'beating'.

Follow the advice about cooking methods, eg 'simmering' is certainly not the same as 'boiling'. Appreciate the importance of good cooking equipment. Modern cookers, such as those illustrated in this book, have so many features that will help you to obtain perfect results.

Jacket Potatoes

4 medium to large potatoes
100g (4oz) cottage cheese
salt and pepper
2tbspn chopped chives

Tomato and Pepper Salad

1 lettuce
8 medium tomatoes
1 green pepper
1 red pepper
French Dressing (see Menu 34)

Mincemeat Apples

4 good-sized cooking apples
4tbspn mincemeat

To Freeze Ahead

Cheese and Tuna Dips freeze well.
Barbecued Chicken: do not freeze the chicken after cooking, but frozen chicken portions can be cooked from frozen.

Safety in Cooking

A barbecue is a good time to stress the importance of perfect safety in cooking. Children love to eat out-of-doors, but make sure there is always an adult around to prevent them going too near the barbecue fire.

A microwave cooker is mentioned in this and other menus in the book and is shown on page 87. This is a very safe method of cooking for the outside of the cooker does not become hot and cooking only begins when the door is shut and the cooker is switched on.

When using the hob of a cooker make sure that all saucepan handles are turned so that no-one passing catches their arm on them. Control the temperature under the saucepan or other pans so the liquid, food or fat does not become too hot. A modern ceramic hob allows a perfect control over the heat.

Choose either a dry white or rosé wine. Look for Greek or Turkish wines to accompany a dish from those countries.

Corn on the Cob
4 corn cobs
salt and pepper
75-100g (3-4oz) butter

Moussaka
2 medium aubergines
4 medium potatoes
2 medium onions
4 medium tomatoes
50g (2oz) butter or margarine
2tbspn oil
salt and pepper
450g (1lb) uncooked lamb or
    beef

For the sauce
75-100g (3-4oz) Gruyère or
    Cheddar cheese
25g (1oz) butter or margarine
25g (1oz) flour
300ml (½pt) milk
1 egg
little grated nutmeg

To garnish
chopped parsley

Variations
1 For a more moist Moussaka
use 40g (1½oz) butter, 40g
(1½oz) flour and 450ml (¾pt)
milk in the sauce, add
150-175g (5-6oz) grated cheese,
seasoning and nutmeg. Put a
little sauce on the meat as well
as the aubergine layers.
2 Use diced cooked meat. It is
a splendid way of of using up
cooked lamb. Shorten the
cooking time by at least 15
minutes.

Green Salad
Use lettuce or endive, watercress, mustard and cress,
cucumber, green pepper,
chicory or celery. Other
ingredients that could be added
are fennel (use the bulb) and
spring onions.

Menu 37   Corn on the Cob

Serves 4   Moussaka
               Green Salad – Tomato Salad

               Lemon Soufflé Pudding

Corn on the Cob
Remove the outer leaves from the cobs. Put into boiling water and boil steadily for 15-20 minutes; remember, over-cooking makes corn tough. Add a little salt towards the end of the cooking period for early salting can add to the toughness of the vegetable.

Melt the butter, add a little salt and pepper to this. It is possible to buy special holders for corn cobs. If you do not possess these, insert fairly thick wooden cocktail sticks into each end of the cooked cob so it can be lifted easily. Spoon the melted butter over the hot cobs.

Serve finger bowls (or pretty soup cups) of cold water; float a small flower head in these, so people can dip their sticky fingers in this before the next course.

Moussaka
Wipe the aubergines (there is advice in Menu 1 for preventing a bitter taste to this vegetable). Peel the potatoes and onions, skin the tomatoes, cut the vegetables into thin slices; keep the onions separate. Heat half the butter or margarine and oil in a pan, fry the onions until soft. Lift on to a plate. Heat the remaining butter or margarine and oil and fry the aubergines with the potatoes for 10 minutes; turn once or twice, season lightly. Mince the meat, blend with the onions and tomatoes, season well.

Grate the cheese. Heat the butter or margarine for the sauce in a pan, stir in the flour, then gradually blend in the milk. Stir as the sauce comes to the boil and thickens over a moderate heat. Add the cheese, salt and pepper. Remove from the heat, whisk in the beaten egg and nutmeg. Put one-third of the aubergines and potatoes into a 1.8 litre (3pt) casserole. Spread with a little sauce. Add half the meat mixture, then half the remaining aubergines and potatoes with a little sauce. Add the rest of the meat mixture. Top with the aubergines, potatoes and a final layer of sauce.

Cover the casserole and cook for 1½ hours in the centre of a very moderate oven, 160°C, 325°F, Gas Mark 3. Remove the lid for the last 20 minutes. Top with the chopped parsley.

Green Salad
If you are being strictly correct, a Green Salad should be just what the title indicates: a collection of green vegetables. It is, however, perfectly all right to add chicory or celery as they have a green tinge, but if tomatoes, etc are included, then immediately you are making a Mixed Salad.

Prepare the various ingredients; do make sure that lettuce and similar salad vegetables are well dried in a salad shaker or gently with kitchen paper or a dry cloth. Shred or leave the leaves whole; blend with all or some of the ingredients suggested.

A good salad depends very much on a well-flavoured dressing. The proportions in Menu 34 are the usual ones. Obviously, you can vary these according to personal taste, but you should consider also the dish with which the salad is being served. In this particular menu I would use less oil as the Moussaka is rich, the ingredients are fried and the dish contains a rich cheese sauce, too. A less oily dressing would, therefore, be more refreshing. Add French Dressing (see Menu 34) to the salad just before serving. Turn the ingredients as you add the dressing so the various ingredients absorb the flavour.

Tomato Salad

Slice the tomatoes thinly, top with a very little lemon juice, herbs, salt and pepper. Leave for about 1 hour before serving.

Lemon Soufflé Pudding

Grate the top yellow 'zest' from the lemons; do not use any bitter pith. Halve the fruit, squeeze out the juice, measure this. In a separate container measure out the milk so you have a *total liquid* content of 200ml (7½fl oz/12tbspn). Cream together the butter or margarine, sugar and lemon rind until soft and light. Separate the eggs; sift together the flour, or flour and baking powder. Gradually beat the egg yolks, then the flour, lemon juice and milk into the creamed fat. The mixture may show signs of curdling, but that does not matter in this particular recipe. Whisk the egg whites until stiff, fold into the lemon mixture, then spoon into a 1 litre (1¾pt) pie or oven-proof dish. Stand this in a bain-marie (dish of cold water). Bake for 50-55 minutes just below the centre of a very moderate oven, 160°C, 325°F, Gas Mark 3, until firm on top. Serve hot. This pudding separates into two layers; the top like a soufflé, the bottom a sauce.

To Make Sunday Easier

1 Prepare Moussaka if not frozen.
2 Prepare chopped parsley and salads; put in refrigerator.

Foods Required

450g (1lb) lamb or beef, 180-205g (8-9oz) butter, 75-100g (3-4oz) Gruyère or Cheddar cheese, 3 eggs, 600ml (1pt) milk (see recipes), 75g (3oz) flour, 50g (2oz) sugar plus pinch (see Lemon Soufflé Pudding), 2tbspn oil, ingredients for French Dressing (see Menu 34), nutmeg, 4 corn cobs, 2 medium aubergines, 4 medium potatoes, 2 medium onions, 4 medium tomatoes, 4 large tomatoes, ingredients for Green Salad, parsley, chives, basil, 2 large lemons plus squeeze of juice.

Packing for a Picnic

There are several menus in this book for eating out of doors and modern insulated boxes and bags enable you to carry a variety of foods easily. These containers also ensure it is kept in perfect condition. Chill the food well before placing it into the container.

You can use the insulated containers to carry hot food, but this must not be mixed with cold dishes.

Tomato Salad

4 large tomatoes
squeeze of lemon juice
1tbspn chopped parsley
1tspn chopped basil
1tspn chopped chives
salt and pepper

Lemon Soufflé Pudding

2 large lemons
milk (see method)
50g (2oz) butter or margarine
50g (2oz) caster sugar*
2 large eggs
50g (2oz) self-raising flour, or
  plain flour with ½tspn
  baking powder

*Increase to personal taste for a sweeter flavour.

Variation
Use the juice and rind of 2 large oranges instead of lemons.

To Freeze Ahead

Moussaka freezes well for 3 months.
Lemon Soufflé Pudding: freeze grated lemon rind and juice when lemons available.

Devilled Mackerel

50g (2oz) butter
1tspn made mustard
1tspn Worcestershire sauce
cayenne pepper and salt
2 large fresh mackerel

Ham and Cheese Cannelloni

12-16 cannelloni tubes
salt and pepper
50g (2oz) butter
50g (2oz) flour
600ml (1pt) milk
1tspn made mustard
225g (8oz) cooked ham
225g (8oz) Cheddar cheese
2tbspn chopped parsley
50g (2oz) soft breadcrumbs

Bean and Cauliflower Salad

1 small cauliflower
350g (12oz) runner beans
French Dressing (see Menu 34)
2tbspn chopped mixed herbs

Rhubarb and Orange Upside Down Pudding

450g (1lb) rhubarb
100g (4oz) butter
175g (6oz) caster sugar
2tspn grated orange rind
4tbspn orange juice
2 eggs
150g (5oz) self-raising flour or plain flour with 1¼tspn baking powder

To Freeze Ahead

Devilled Mackerel: use frozen mackerel.
Cannelloni: prepare and freeze.
Rhubarb and Orange Upside Down Pudding: cook and freeze.

Menu 38

Serves 4

Devilled Mackerel

Ham and Cheese Cannelloni
Bean and Cauliflower Salad

Rhubarb and Orange Upside Down Pudding

Devilled Mackerel

Blend together the butter, mustard, Worcestershire sauce, pepper and salt. Fillet the fish; place the 4 fillets on a flat oven-proof dish, top with the butter mixture. Bake for 15 minutes towards the top of a moderate oven, 180°C, 350°F, Gas Mark 4. Serve with brown bread and butter.

Ham and Cheese Cannelloni

Cook the cannelloni in boiling salted water; drain. Heat the butter in a pan, stir in the flour, cook gently for 2-3 minutes; add the milk, stir as the sauce comes to the boil and thickens, season to taste. Mince or finely chop the ham, grate the cheese. Mix together the ham, 175g (6oz) of the cheese, parsley and one-third of the sauce. Insert into the cannelloni tubes. Pour a little sauce into a casserole, top with the cannelloni and remaining sauce, then the breadcrumbs and the rest of the cheese. Cook for 35 minutes in the centre of a moderate oven.

Bean and Cauliflower Salad

Divide the cauliflower into florets; slice the beans. Cook in boiling salted water; drain and mix with the dressing and herbs.

Rhubarb and Orange Upside Down Pudding

Firm autumn rhubarb is ideal. Cut into neat pieces. Spread 25g (1oz) butter in the bottom of a 20cm (8in) soufflé dish, add the rhubarb, half the sugar, half the orange rind and 1tbspn orange juice. Cream the rest of the butter, sugar and orange rind, beat in the eggs. Sift the flour, or flour and baking powder, fold into the creamed mixture with the 3tbspn orange juice. Spoon over the rhubarb. Bake for 1 hour in the centre of a moderate oven. Serve with cream.

To Make Sunday Easier

1 Prepare cannelloni dish ready to cook. Make the salad.
2 Make, but do not bake, the dessert. Cover, put in the refrigerator.

Foods Required

225g (8oz) cooked ham, 2 large fresh mackerel, 200g (8oz) butter plus extra for spreading, 225g (8oz) Cheddar cheese, 150ml (¼pt) single or double cream, 2 eggs, 600ml (1pt) milk, 200g (7oz) flour, 1 brown loaf and bread to give 50g (2oz) breadcrumbs, 175g (6oz) caster sugar, 12-16 cannelloni tubes, Worcestershire sauce, cayenne pepper, mustard, ingredients for French Dressing (see Menu 34), 1 small cauliflower, 350g (12oz) runner beans, mixed herbs including parsley, 450g (1lb) rhubarb, 2 oranges.

Menu 39
Stuffed Peppers; Curried Eggs with Rice and Accompaniments

Stuffed Peppers
2 medium green peppers
2 medium red peppers
salt

For the stuffing
225g (8oz) Cheddar cheese
50g (2oz) breadcrumbs
50g (2oz) cream cheese
2tbspn chopped walnuts
2tbspn sultanas
1 egg

3tbspn crisp breadcrumbs
25g (1oz) margarine

Home-made Rolls
0.5kg (generous 1lb) strong flour
½ level tspn salt or to taste
15g (½oz) fresh yeast or 1½ level tspn dried yeast and 1tspn sugar (see method)
approximately 300ml (½pt) water

Variations
1 Use wholemeal flour instead of white, in which case you will need a little more liquid to make a more moist dough.
2 Rub 25g (1oz) fat into the flour.
3 Milk rolls: mix with milk instead of water.
4 If more convenient, prepare the dough, make the rolls overnight, cover the trays, put in the refrigerator for very slow 'proving'. If insufficiently risen, leave at room temperature for a time (see opposite), then bake.

Menu 39	Stuffed Peppers with Home-made Rolls
Serves 4	Curried Eggs with Rice and Accompaniments
	Damson Amber

Stuffed Peppers
Halve the peppers lengthways (they stand better this way). Carefully remove the cores and seeds. Put into boiling salted water for 5 minutes, then drain. Grate the cheese and blend three-quarters of this with the other ingredients for the stuffing. Spoon into the halved peppers; place in a greased oven-proof dish. Top each halved pepper with the crisp breadcrumbs and remaining cheese. Melt the margarine, spoon over the topping. Bake for 25-30 minutes in the centre of a moderate oven, 180°C, 350°F, Gas Mark 4. Serve hot.

Home-made Rolls
Sift the flour and salt into a warm mixing bowl.

Cream fresh yeast in a basin, warm the water to blood heat, pour over the yeast and mix thoroughly.

If using dried yeast, warm the water, add the sugar, sprinkle the dried yeast on top and leave for about 10 minutes, then follow directions for fresh yeast.

Make a well in the centre of the flour, pour in the yeast liquid, put a sprinkling of flour over the top and leave until frothy, then blend the ingredients together to form a soft ball. The mixing bowl should be left clean. Makes of flour vary in the amount of liquid they absorb, so you may need either a little more flour or a very little more liquid.

Turn the dough on to a floured surface and knead thoroughly. This process means pulling the dough towards you, then pushing it away with the base of the palm of the hand (called the 'heel'). Continue until the dough is smooth. Return to the bowl; cover with a cloth. Leave in a warm but not hot place—the airing cupboard or near the cooker is a good choice—for about 1 hour, or until the dough has *just* doubled in size. Turn on to a floured board again and knead as before. To test if adequately kneaded, press the dough with a floured finger. This will leave an impression; if it comes out the dough is adequately kneaded.

Divide into 12-14 small pieces, shape into neat rounds or desired shapes. Put on to lightly greased baking trays; allow room to spread as well as rise. If possible, slip the trays into large greased polythene bags so the dough does not develop a crust before cooking. It is not essential to cover the rolls. Allow to rise until nearly double the original size; this takes about 15 minutes. Remove from the bags.

Bake for 12-15 minutes towards the top of a hot to very hot oven, 220-230°C, 425-450°F, Gas Mark 7-8.

Curried Eggs

Peel and chop the onion and apple. Heat the margarine in a pan and cook the onion and apple until nearly soft; blend in the curry powder and cornflour. Stir over a low heat for 2-3 minutes, then add the water, tomato juice and bring to the boil. Stir until slightly thickened, then add the sultanas, lemon juice, chutney, coconut, salt and pepper to taste. Simmer gently for about 30 minutes in a covered saucepan.

Meanwhile, hard-boil and shell the eggs. If you can allow these to stand in the sauce (without cooking) for 1-2 hours they absorb the curry flavour. This prevents over-cooking the eggs. Heat gently just before required.

Serve in a border of cooked rice (see Menu 32); garnish with small pieces of red pepper and green peas. Accompany with dishes of chutney, sliced bananas, raisins, sliced tomatoes, gherkins, cocktail onions and salted peanuts.

Damson Amber

Simmer the damsons with the water and sugar to taste until soft. Sieve, then blend with the cake crumbs. Separate the eggs, beat the yolks into the mixture. Taste and adjust the sweetness if necessary. Put into a 900ml (1½pt) pie dish and bake for approximately 45 minutes in the centre of a very moderate oven, 160°C, 325°F, Gas Mark 3, until firm to the touch. Whisk the egg whites until stiff; fold in 50g (2oz) sugar. Spoon over the top of the mixture. Return to the oven, lower the heat to cool, 150°C, 300°F, Gas Mark 2. Serve hot.

To Make Sunday Easier

1 Make and bake rolls day beforehand if not freezing these; reheat on Sunday.
2 Prepare Stuffed Peppers. Do not put on topping; cover with clingfilm or foil and store in refrigerator. Add topping just before cooking.
3 Cook Curry Sauce a day or so beforehand; reheat on Sunday and add eggs, or put hard-boiled eggs into the cold Curry Sauce late on Saturday, then reheat.
4 Prepare damson purée and blend with the crumbs and egg yolks. Put into pie dish, cover and store in refrigerator.

Foods Required

75g (3oz) margarine, 225g (8oz) Cheddar cheese, 50g (2oz) cream cheese, 11 eggs, 0.5kg (1lb) strong flour, 15g (½oz) fresh yeast or 1½tspn dried yeast, approximately 150g (5oz) caster sugar, bread to give 50g (2oz) breadcrumbs, 3tbspn crisp breadcrumbs, sponge to give 50g (2oz) crumbs, 1tbspn cornflour, 150ml (¼pt) tomato juice, 175g (6oz) long grain rice, 2tbspn walnuts, 4tbspn sultanas, smooth chutney, 1tbspn desiccated coconut, 1tbspn curry powder, accompaniments to Curried Eggs (see method), 1 large onion, 2 medium red peppers, 2 medium green peppers, few frozen peas, 550-675g (1¼-1½lb) damsons, 1 small dessert apple, lemon for 1tbspn lemon juice.

Curried Eggs

1 large onion
1 small dessert apple
50g (2oz) margarine
1tbspn curry powder
1tbspn cornflour
300ml (½pt) water
150ml (¼pt) tomato juice
2tbspn sultanas
1tbspn lemon juice
1tbspn smooth chutney
1tbspn desiccated coconut
salt and pepper
8 eggs

175g (6oz) long grain rice

To garnish
diced red pepper
cooked peas
accompaniments (see method)

Damson Amber

550-675g (1¼-1½lb) damsons
2-3tbspn water
approximately 150g (5oz) caster sugar
50g (2oz) fine soft cake crumbs
2 eggs

Variation
For a more substantial sweet, bake a flan first, put in the filling and continue as above.

To Freeze Ahead

Stuffed Peppers: prepare and freeze without topping, add this when defrosted rather than cooking then freezing.
Rolls freeze well.
Curried Eggs: freeze the sauce, but never freeze hard-boiled eggs.
Damson Amber: either freeze the damson purée or bake, then freeze the fruit mixture at the base of the pudding. Allow to defrost, warm through in the oven, top with the meringue and complete cooking as recipe.

If you use red wine in the Pot Roast, serve this with the meal. A Rhône wine such as Hermitage would be excellent.

Creamed Spinach Soup

1 medium onion
50g (2oz) butter
25g (1oz) flour
600ml (1pt) milk or 450ml
   (¾pt) milk and 150ml (¼pt)
   single cream
salt and pepper
350g (12oz) spinach
little chicken stock or extra
   milk (see method)
little grated nutmeg

Pot Roast of Beef with Mixed Vegetables

450g (1lb) medium onions
450g (1lb) medium carrots
1 head of celery
50g (2oz) fat
1.3-1.5kg (3-3½lb) topside of
   beef
bouquet garni
salt and pepper
beef stock (see method)

450g (1lb) medium potatoes

Variation
Use a little red wine instead of some of the stock.

Runner beans

675g (1½lb) runner beans
salt

Pears Belle Helene

Chocolate Sauce (see Menu 49)
Ice-cream (see Menu 18)
6 canned or fresh ripe dessert
   pear halves

To Freeze Ahead

Spinach Soup: freeze spinach purée and thicken after defrosting.
Pot Roast of Beef: if using frozen beef, defrost before cooking and dry well.
Pears Belle Helene: dessert pears can be frozen in syrup, but their flavour and texture is not as good as canned or bottled.

Menu 40

Serves 6

Creamed Spinach Soup

Pot Roast of Beef with Mixed Vegetables
Runner Beans

Pears Belle Helene

Creamed Spinach Soup

Peel and finely chop the onion. Heat the butter in a pan, add the onion, cook until tender; do not brown. Blend in the flour, then gradually add the milk, or milk and cream. Bring to the boil, stir until a smooth thin sauce, season lightly. Meanwhile, wash and cook the spinach as described in Menu 1, then sieve or finely chop. Blend with the sauce; if necessary, add extra stock or milk to make the right consistency. Adjust the seasoning, add nutmeg. Serve with croûtons (see Menu 44).

Pot Roast of Beef with Mixed Vegetables

Peel the onions and carrots; keep whole. Wash and dice the celery. Heat the fat in a large saucepan, put in the meat, brown well, then remove from the pan. Add the onions and carrots, turn in the fat until lightly browned. Pour off any surplus fat; add the celery, bouquet garni, seasoning and stock to barely cover the vegetables. Place the meat on top of the vegetables. Put on a tight-fitting lid. Bring the liquid to simmering point, cook steadily. Allow 25-30 minutes per 450g (1lb). Peel the potatoes, add to the pan 35-40 minutes before end of cooking time. Season and check there is enough liquid. If more convenient, cook Pot Roast in a covered casserole in a very moderate oven, 160°C, 325°F, Gas Mark 3, for nearly 3 hours.

Serve the meat with the vegetables. The liquid in the pan makes a delicious gravy. Any vegetables left over can be used in a soup.

Runner beans: string and slice, cook steadily in boiling salted water.

Pears Belle Helene

Make the Chocolate Sauce. Spoon the ice-cream into sundae glasses. Top with the halved pears and the Chocolate Sauce.

To Make Sunday Easier

1   Make soup completely on Saturday; keep in covered container.
2   Prepare vegetables; keep in cold water in cool place.
3   Freeze ice-cream when convenient (see Menu 18).

Foods Required

1.3-1.5kg (3-3½lb) topside of beef, 115g (4½oz) butter, 50g (2oz) fat, 300ml (½pt) whipping or double cream, 2 large eggs, 600ml (1pt) milk plus 6tbspn or 450ml (¾pt) milk and 150ml (¼pt) single cream plus 6tbspn, 25g (1oz) flour, 25g (1oz) caster sugar, 50g (2oz) icing sugar, 2-3 slices bread, 175g (6oz) plain chocolate, vanilla essence, nutmeg, 6 canned or ripe dessert pears, 450g (1lb) medium onions plus 1, 450g (1lb) medium carrots, 450g (1lb) medium potatoes, 350g (12oz) spinach, 1 head celery, fresh herbs for bouquet garni, 675g (1½lb) runner beans.

Menu 7

Steak and Kidney Pudding, Parsley Potatoes, Carrot Sticks, Haricot Verts; Dried Fruit Compôte

Piperade

1 small onion
2 medium tomatoes
1 small green pepper
50g (2oz) butter or margarine
salt and pepper
4 eggs
1tbspn chopped parsley
4 slices of bread

Veal Cordon Bleu

4 veal escalopes
4 thin slices cooked ham
4 thin slices Gruyère or
   Cheddar cheese

To coat
salt and pepper
1tbspn flour
1 egg
50g (2oz) fine soft breadcrumbs

For frying
50g (2oz) butter
2tbspn oil

To garnish
lemon wedges, watercress

Variation
Wiener Schnitzel: coat the thin
fillets of veal with crisp breadcrumbs, fry and top with
chopped hard-boiled egg,
parsley and anchovy fillet.

Piquant Sauce

425g (15oz) can plum tomatoes
salt and pepper
2tspn French mustard
1tspn Worcestershire sauce

Menu 41	Piperade
Serves 4	Veal Cordon Bleu with Piquant Sauce
	Golden Creamed Potatoes — Leeks
	Banana and Orange Creams

Piperade

Peel and finely chop the onion. Skin and chop the tomatoes. Cut the pepper into small dice; discard core and seeds. Heat the butter or margarine in a saucepan, add the vegetables, fry until soft. Season and beat the eggs, add to the pan with the parsley. Scramble until lightly set. Meanwhile, toast the bread. Serve the mixture on or with hot toast. This dish is very good cold; remember in this case to cook very lightly as the eggs become firmer as they cool.

Veal Cordon Bleu

Beat the veal with a dampened rolling pin or between two sheets of greaseproof paper until about twice the size of the slices of ham and cheese. Place the ham and cheese on the veal so they cover only half the meat. Fold the uncovered veal over to form a sandwich. Season the flour with a little salt and pepper, dust the meat with this. Beat the egg, brush over the veal, then coat with the crumbs. As the frying time for this particular dish is relatively long, soft breadcrumbs are advisable. Heat the butter and oil in a large frying pan; fry the veal on either side until crisp and brown. Lower the heat and cook for a further 6-7 minutes. Garnish with the lemon and watercress.

Piquant Sauce

Liquidise or sieve the canned tomatoes. Put into the saucepan with salt, pepper, mustard and Worcestershire sauce. Heat until a fairly thick purée. This sauce is nicer if not thickened with flour.

Golden Creamed Potatoes

Peel the potatoes; cook in boiling salted water until just cooked. Strain, return to the pan and mash. Meanwhile, peel and finely grate the carrots, add to the hot potatoes. Heat the butter or margarine and milk, gradually beat into the potato and carrot mixture; heat gently as you beat. Taste and add any extra seasoning required.

Leeks

Trim the tough green tops from the leeks. Put the vegetable into cold water and gently pull apart the folds to wash off the fine dirt that lurks there; wash thoroughly; change the water once or twice if necessary. Heat only about 3.5-5cm (1½-2in) water in a large saucepan. It is much easier to cook leeks well if they form a fairly shallow layer in the pan. Add a good pinch of salt, then put the leeks into the boiling water. Lower the heat and cook steadily until just tender. This particular vegetable is nicer if it has a slightly firm texture. Strain and arrange in a dish; top with the chopped parsley.

Banana and Orange Creams

Dissolve the jelly in the hot water. Allow to cool, add the cold orange juice. Skin and mash the bananas with the lemon juice and sugar. Blend with the cold jelly. This could be done in a liquidiser (blender) or food processor if preferred; it gives a smoother mixture. Allow to cool and just begin to stiffen. Whip the cream lightly, fold half into the banana and orange mixture. Spoon into individual dishes; leave until set, then top with the rest of the whipped cream and the flaked almonds.

To Make Sunday Easier

1   Lightly cook the vegetable mixture for Piperade; put into a basin and cover. If you have a microwave cooker, add the eggs to the warmed vegetable mixture on Sunday; scramble in the basin.
2   Prepare the Veal Cordon Bleu the night beforehand; the coating adheres better to the meat when frying this if it is really well chilled. Make Piquant Sauce if this is not being frozen.
3   Make the Banana and Orange Creams.

Foods Required

4 veal escalopes, 4 thin slices cooked ham, 125g (5oz) butter, 4 thin slices Gruyère or Cheddar cheese, 150ml (¼pt) double cream, 5 eggs, 3tbspn milk, 1tbspn flour, 25g (1oz) caster sugar, bread to give 4 slices and 50g (2oz) breadcrumbs, 2tbspn oil, 425g (15oz) can plum tomatoes, French mustard, 1tspn Worcestershire sauce, 1 orange jelly, 150ml (¼pt) orange juice, 25g (1oz) flaked blanched almonds, 1 small onion, 2 medium tomatoes, 2 medium carrots, 1 small green pepper, watercress, 450-675g (1-1½lb) potatoes, 8 medium leeks, parsley, 1-2 lemons, 2 large ripe unblemished bananas.

Choice of Cheese in a Menu

Dairies, grocers and supermarkets have an almost bewildering choice of cheese, for we not only produce our own cheeses but import many kinds from the countries of the world.

An interesting cheese board need not have an enormous number of cheeses, but it should offer a variety of flavours and textures. Select from the following:

a)   A hard firm cheese, such as Cheddar, Cheshire, Double Gloucester from Britain; Port Salut from France; Edam or Gouda from Holland. Look out for lesser known cheeses, such as Cotswold Cheese with Chives; Sage Derby (where the cheese is flavoured with sage leaves).
b)   A soft creamy cheese such as Caerphilly from Britain; Livarot, Demi-Sel, Brie, Camembert from France or the delicious Campazola (veined Brie); Ricotta from Italy is a beautifully soft rich cheese; Limburger from Germany, and Feta from Greece.
c)   Strongly flavoured veined cheeses include Stilton from Britain, Rocquefort and Gorgonzola from France; Danish Blue from Denmark, and the soft, but definite-flavoured Dolcelatte from Italy.

Golden Creamed Potatoes

450-675g (1-1½lb) potatoes
salt and pepper
2 medium carrots
25g (1oz) butter or margarine
3tbspn milk

Leeks

8 medium leeks (try and buy them all the same thickness to facilitate easy cooking)
salt

To garnish
chopped parsley

Banana and Orange Creams

1 orange jelly
300ml (½pt) hot water
150ml (¼pt) orange juice
2 large ripe unblemished bananas
2tbspn lemon juice
25g (1oz) caster sugar
150ml (¼pt) double cream
25g (1oz) flaked blanched almonds

Variations
1 Omit orange juice; use 450ml (¾pt) water.
2 Use 15g (½oz) gelatine with 450ml (¾pt) fresh orange juice; increase sugar to 50g (2oz).

To Freeze Ahead

Piperade: if you are fond of this dish, cook large quantities of the vegetable mixture, divide into required amounts and freeze.
Veal Cordon Bleu can be prepared and frozen, although veal is the least successful meat for freezing.
Piquant Sauce freezes for up to 6 months.

A well-chilled lager would be refreshing with the chicken or have a dry white wine.

Liver and Cottage Cheese Pâté

175g (6oz) liver pâté (see Menu 33) or use soft liver sausage
175g (6oz) cottage cheese
2tspn chopped chives
1tspn chopped parsley
salt, pepper and garlic salt

To garnish
lettuce, gherkins, lemon wedges

Devilled Spatchcock of Chicken

4 small or 2 large spring chickens (poussin)
50g (2oz) butter or 2tbspn oil
1tspn Worcestershire sauce
few drops Tabasco sauce
1tspn made mustard
pinch curry powder
salt and pepper

Peas and Sweetcorn

675g (1½lb) fresh peas
salt
mint
175g (6oz) canned sweetcorn
knob of butter

Fruit Gâteau

sponge cake (see Menu 30)
450g (1lb) strawberries or other fruit
sugar to taste
150-300ml (¼-½pt) whipping cream

To Freeze Ahead

Spatchcock of Chicken: split chickens before freezing; they can then be cooked from frozen.
Fruit Gâteau: if you like a moist gâteau, fill and decorate before freezing. For a drier texture, freeze sponges, then fill and decorate after defrosting. Open-freeze, then pack.

Menu 42	Liver and Cottage Cheese Pâté
Serves 4	Devilled Spatchcock of Chicken Peas and Sweetcorn
	Fruit Gâteau

Liver and Cottage Cheese Pâté
Put the pâté or liver sausage into a basin. Sieve the cottage cheese. Add these to the other ingredients and mix thoroughly. Spoon on to crisp lettuce, garnish with the gherkins (cut into fan shapes) and lemon. Serve with hot toast and butter.

Devilled Spatchcock of Chicken
Split the chickens down their backs so the birds can be flattened. Melt the butter or warm the oil; blend with the two sauces, the mustard, curry powder, salt and pepper. Brush the birds with the flavoured butter and cook under a pre-heated grill for about 15 minutes until tender. Brush once or twice with the butter mixture during cooking.

Peas and Sweetcorn
Shell the peas, put into boiling, lightly salted water. Add a sprig of mint, cook steadily for 8-10 minutes. Add well-drained sweetcorn towards the end of the cooking time. Strain, top with the butter.

Fruit Gâteau
Put the bottom layer of sponge on a dish. Slice half the fruit, put on the sponge with a sprinkling of sugar. Whip the cream, spread half over the fruit. Top with the second layer of sponge, remaining cream and fruit.

To Make Sunday Easier
1 Make pâté a day beforehand; cover well to prevent drying. This pâté is too delicate in flavour to be covered with melted butter.
2 Cut chicken ready for cooking. If the weather is suitable and you have a barbecue fire, cook outside.
3 Make the gâteau a day beforehand. If filling and decorating, put in a covered container in the refrigerator so the cream does not dry. The flavour of the gâteau is better if prepared ahead.

Foods Required
4 small or 2 large spring chickens (poussin), 50g (2oz) butter or 2tbspn oil plus knob of butter and butter for toast, 175g (6oz) cottage cheese, 175g (6oz) liver pâté (see Menu 33) or soft liver sausage, 150-300ml (¼-½pt) whipping cream, 3 large eggs, 75g (3oz) flour, 100g (4oz) sugar plus little extra, bread for toast, 1tspn Worcestershire sauce, Tabasco sauce, mustard, garlic salt, gherkins, curry powder, 175g (6oz) canned sweetcorn, 675g (1½lb) fresh peas, lettuce, chives, parsley, mint, 1 lemon, 450g (1lb) strawberries.

Menu 20
Smoked and Fresh Salmon Mousse; Roast Duckling with Apricot Sauce, Rillette of Duck, Mashed Turnips, Mange Tout Peas; Citrus Fruit Salad

Barbecued Spare Ribs

2kg (4-4½lb) pork spare ribs
1tbspn brown malt vinegar
pinch ground ginger
1 medium onion
1 garlic clove
salt and pepper

For the sauce
1 medium onion
1tbspn oil
1½tspn cornflour
6tbspn brown malt vinegar
150ml (¼pt) stock (see method)
4tbspn pineapple syrup
   (from canned fruit)
1tbspn brown sugar
1-2tbspn apricot or plum or
   pineapple jam
1tbspn soy sauce
salt and pepper
¼tspn ground ginger

Cheese and Haddock Soufflé

150g (5oz) cooked smoked
   haddock
75g (3oz) Cheddar cheese
25g (1oz) butter or margarine
25g (1oz) flour
150ml (¼pt) milk
4tbspn single cream or extra
   milk
pinch mustard powder
shake cayenne pepper
salt and pepper
1tspn grated lemon rind
1tbspn chopped parsley
3 eggs
1 egg white

Tomato and Green Pepper Salad

1 lettuce
4 large tomatoes
1 large green pepper
2tbspn chopped spring onions
1tbspn chopped parsley
2tbspn French Dressing (see
   Menu 34)

Menu 43

Serves 4-6

Barbecued Spare Ribs

Cheese and Haddock Soufflé
Tomato and Green Pepper Salad

Yoghurt and Fresh Fruit

Barbecued Spare Ribs

Ask the butcher for spare ribs for the Chinese method of cooking so he produces the bones with a limited amount of meat and cut into neat pieces.

Put the spare ribs into a saucepan, cover with cold water, add the 1tbspn vinegar and ginger. Peel the onion and garlic clove, put into the liquid with salt and pepper to taste. Bring this to simmering point, cover the pan and simmer for 25 minutes, strain and save 150ml (¼pt) of the liquid. Dry the bones well on absorbent paper. Put in a flat layer in a roasting tin and cook for 25 minutes in the centre of a hot oven, 220°C, 425°F, Gas Mark 7; after this time lower the heat to moderate, 180°C, 350°F, Gas Mark 4, and continue cooking for a further 10 minutes before adding the sauce.

To make the sauce, peel and finely chop the onion; heat the oil in a large frying pan, fry the onion until tender. Blend the cornflour with the 6tbspn vinegar and the reserved stock. Add the rest of the ingredients; stir over a low heat until thickened and smooth. Pour over the spare ribs; turn these in the sauce so they become well coated. Continue cooking for a further 10-15 minutes. You may need to move the roasting tin in the oven for this period to accommodate the soufflé dish in the centre of the oven. Serve any sauce left in the tin with the spare ribs.

Cheese and Haddock Soufflé

Grease a 15-18cm (6-7in) soufflé dish. Flake the fish and grate the cheese. Heat the butter or margarine in a large saucepan, add the flour, stir over the heat for 2-3 minutes, then gradually blend in the milk, or milk and cream. Stir as the sauce comes to the boil and thickens. Add the seasonings, lemon rind and parsley; be sparing with the salt, then remove the pan from the heat. Separate the eggs, beat the yolks, fish and cheese into the sauce. Whisk the 4 egg whites until stiff, fold into the mixture in the saucepan. Pour into the soufflé dish and bake in the centre of a moderate oven, 180°C, 350°F, Gas Mark 4, for 35-40 minutes or until well risen and golden. Serve at once.

Tomato and Green Pepper Salad

Shred the lettuce. Slice the tomatoes; discard the core and seeds of the green pepper, slice; arrange on the lettuce. Add the remaining ingredients.

Yoghurt and Fresh Fruit

For an informal meal leave commercial yoghurt in the containers. For a more attractive presentation, brush the rims of sundae glasses with a little unwhisked egg white, then dip in caster sugar. Leave to harden, then spoon in the yoghurt.

To Make Sunday Easier
1 Prepare the ingredients for the sauce in which to cook the Barbecued Spare Ribs.
2 Grate the cheese; cook and flake the fish for the soufflé (keep both cheese and fish well covered to prevent drying).
3 Decorate the rims of the sundae glasses for the dessert (see recipe).

Foods Required
2kg (4-4½lb) pork spare ribs, 225g (8oz) smoked haddock to give 150g (5oz) when cooked, 25g (1oz) butter or margarine, 75g (3oz) Cheddar cheese, 4tbspn single cream or extra milk, 4 eggs (3 yolks only used), 150ml (¼pt) milk, 600-900ml (1-1½pt) yoghurt, 25g (1oz) flour, 1tbspn brown sugar, 1tbspn oil, 1½tspn cornflour, 4tbspn pineapple syrup (from canned fruit), 1-2tbspn apricot or plum or pineapple jam, soy sauce, mustard, cayenne pepper, 7tbspn brown malt vinegar, ground ginger, oil and vinegar for French Dressing (see Menu 34), 2 medium onions, few spring onions, 1 garlic clove, lettuce, 4 large tomatoes, 1 large green pepper, parsley, 1 lemon, fresh fruit.

Salads and Vegetables
Salads and vegetables play a large part in making a meal enjoyable. Over the years we have altered a great deal in the way we like vegetables cooked; they should be firm in texture so they retain not only their flavour but their vitamin value too (see below).

Often the meal is better balanced if you serve a crisp salad with a hot main course instead of or with hot vegetables.

Cooking Green Vegetables (and Red Cabbage)
Do not spoil a good meal by cooking green vegetables less than perfectly. Prepare the vegetables just before a meal; soaking them in water destroys valuable vitamins. For best results:

a) Use the minimum amount of water, which also means a relatively small quantity of salt is needed.
b) Make sure the water is boiling when adding the vegetables and add these steadily so the water returns to boiling in the shortest possible time.
c) Do not over-cook the vegetables; they taste and look so much better when lightly cooked. Also, they retain more of their vitamin value.

Cooking Root Vegetables and Pulses
Details on cooking potatoes well are given in Menu 7, but remember other root vegetables should be cooked steadily, rather than too quickly.

Peas and beans (the pulses) should also be cooked steadily, rather than boiled rapidly. French beans and haricots verts are generally cooked whole; just remove the tougher ends, and string (remove the side parts) only if these seem tough. Runner beans need stringing and slicing before cooking.

Yoghurt and Fresh Fruit
Allow 150ml (¼pt) plain or flavoured yoghurt per person with a selection of fruit in season.

To Freeze Ahead
The various dishes in this menu are unsuitable for freezing, but it is quite a good idea to ask the butcher for spare ribs when these are available—you cannot always obtain them just when required. They freeze well, but you must defrost them before-hand and dry them well on absorbent paper so they will crisp. Use pork spare ribs within 6 months.
Cheese and Haddock Soufflé: when you have a surplus of Cheddar or other hard cheese, grate and store in containers in the freezer.
Smoked haddock can be kept in the freezer. It is better if uncooked.
Green peppers can be frozen as other vegetables, ie by blanching whole, diced or sliced; freeze or open-freeze, then wrap. However, they do lose their crisp texture.

Decorating Dishes
The recipe for serving the yoghurt suggests decorating the rim of the sundae glasses. The frosted effect of egg white then caster or sieved icing sugar can be used for a number of sweet dishes.

When serving cold soups, you can adapt the idea by dipping the rim of the soup cup or dish in water or lightly whisked egg white and coating it with finely chopped parsley.

This is perhaps slightly more of an informal lunch than a brunch for it starts with soup. You could have a dry sherry or very cold beer.

Golden Stilton Soup

1 medium onion
2 medium carrots
50g (2oz) butter
25g (1oz) flour
300ml (½pt) milk
450ml (¾pt) chicken stock
175g (6oz) Stilton cheese
4tbspn cream
salt and pepper
pinch dry mustard

Fried Croûtons

2-3 slices of bread
50g (2oz) butter

Kedgeree

450g (1lb) smoked haddock
  (weight without skin and
  bones)
175g (6oz) long grain rice
450ml (¾pt) water
salt and pepper
2-3 eggs
50g (2oz) butter or margarine
4tbspn single cream
1tbspn chopped parsley
4-8 large tomatoes

Apple and Orange Compôte

150ml (¼pt) water
50-75g (2-3oz) sugar
3 oranges
450g (1lb) cooking apples
600ml (1pt) yoghurt

To Freeze Ahead

Stilton Soup: do not over-cook when reheating. Freeze and use within 2 months.
Croûtons, see Menu 5.
Kedgeree: freeze without eggs; add when reheating with a little cream. Use within 6 weeks.
Apple and Orange Compôte: cook and freeze apples with orange rind.

Golden Stilton Soup – Fried Croûtons

Kedgeree

Apple and Orange Compôte

Golden Stilton Soup

Peel and finely chop the onion; peel and grate the carrots. Heat the butter, add the onion and cook for 2-3 minutes; stir in the flour, then blend in the milk and stock. Bring to the boil over a moderate heat, stir until thickened, then simmer for 10 minutes. Add the Stilton cheese, cream, salt, pepper, mustard and the grated carrots. Heat until the cheese has melted. Serve with Fried Croûtons.

Fried Croûtons

Cut the bread into 0.5cm (¼in) dice; do not use the crusts. Heat the butter and fry the bread until crisp. Drain on absorbent paper.

Kedgeree

Poach the haddock in water until tender, drain and then flake the fish. Meanwhile, put the rice into the cold water, add a little salt. Bring to the boil, stir briskly with a fork; cover the saucepan and allow the rice to simmer for 15 minutes or until tender. Hard-boil the eggs. Shell these and chop the whites and yolks separately. Heat the butter or margarine in a large saucepan, add the fish and rice and then the cream. Heat thoroughly, stir in the chopped egg whites. Spoon the fish mixture into a neat shape on a heated dish and top with the chopped egg yolk and parsley. Meanwhile, halve, season and grill the tomatoes. Arrange around the kedgeree.

Apple and Orange Compôte

Put the water and sugar into a saucepan. Grate just the top 'zest' from the oranges, add to the water, heat until the sugar has dissolved. Peel and slice the apples, poach in the orange-flavoured syrup until tender, then cool. Cut out the orange segments; discard any skin, pith and pips. Add to the apples. Serve with yoghurt.

To Make Sunday Easier

1 Make soup, but reheat carefully. Fry croûtons; reheat in oven.
2 Prepare ingredients for Kedgeree; cover well to prevent drying.
3 Make compôte.

Foods Required

450g (1lb) smoked haddock, 150g (6oz) butter, 175g (6oz) Stilton cheese, 8tbspn single cream, 2-3 eggs, 300ml (½pt) milk, 600ml (1pt) yoghurt, 25g (1oz) flour, 50-75g (2-3oz) sugar, 2-3 slices bread, mustard, 175g (6oz) long grain rice, 1 medium onion, 2 medium carrots, 4-8 large tomatoes, parsley, 3 oranges, 450g (1lb) cooking apples.

Menu 43
Cheese and Haddock Soufflé

This menu provides a good
opportunity to try red wines
from less-known sources, such as
Hungary. A Spanish red wine
from the Rioja or Penedés areas
would be another wise choice.

Menu 45

Serves 4

Lofoten Caviar

Beef Olives
Creamed Potatoes — Macedoine of Vegetables

Apricot Coconut Streusel

Lofoten Caviar

450g (1lb) uncooked cod's roe
150ml (¼pt) water or strained
   fish stock
salt and pepper
1tspn sugar
2 eggs
2-4tbspn olive or salad oil
2tbspn lemon juice
1 garlic clove or little garlic salt

Variation
After boiling, cool and slice the
cod's roe and fry in butter.
Serve with lemon.

Beef Olives

4 large slices topside of beef
stuffing as Forcemeat Balls, but
   use 1 whole egg instead of
   just egg yolk (see Menu 5)

For the sauce
25g (1oz) flour
salt and pepper
50g (2oz) fat or beef dripping
450ml (¾pt) beef stock
1 bay leaf

To garnish
Macedoine of Vegetables

Creamed Potatoes

450-675g (1-1½lb) old potatoes
salt and pepper
25-50g (1-2oz) butter or
   margarine
2-3tbspn milk

Lofoten Caviar

Put the cod's roe into the water or stock, add a little salt, pepper and the sugar. Leave for about 2 hours. This softens the fish and makes it more moist when cooked. Simmer the roe in the water in which it was soaked for 15-20 minutes until it turns white in colour. Strain and make the 'caviar' at once. Hard-boil the eggs. Skin and mash the roe, then gradually beat in the oil; the larger amount is traditional, but it may make the dish too oily for many people, so add the oil slowly and adjust the amount to personal taste. Beat in the lemon juice. Peel the garlic clove and crush, or squeeze out the juice through a garlic press. Add the crushed garlic or garlic juice or garlic salt to the other ingredients. Taste and add desired amount of seasoning. Shell the eggs; chop the whites and yolks separately. Spoon the cod's roe into individual dishes; top with a ring of egg white, then a ring of egg yolk. Serve with wedges of lemon, hot toast and butter.

   This is too generous an amount of 'caviar' for 4 people, but any roe left over can be covered and stored in the refrigerator for a few days, or frozen (see freezing instructions).

Beef Olives

Flatten each slice of beef with a damp rolling pin, then cut into half, so giving 8 slices. Prepare the stuffing as described in Menu 5. Divide this between the slices of meat. The term 'olives' came from the fact that the meat was gathered around the stuffing to form a round, but nowadays it is usual to roll the meat around the stuffing. Secure with fine string, cotton or wooden cocktail sticks. Blend the flour with the salt and pepper and coat the meat rolls. Heat the fat or dripping in a pan and brown the meat, then lift into a casserole. Blend the stock with the meat juices in the pan, add the bay leaf, stir well, then pour over the meat. Cover the casserole and cook for 1½ hours in the centre of a very moderate oven, 160°C, 325°F, Gas Mark 3. Lift the meat rolls on to a dish, remove the string or cotton or cocktail sticks. Pour some of the sauce over the beef; the rest should be put into a sauce boat. Arrange the Macedoine of Vegetables round the edge of the dish.

Creamed Potatoes

Follow the directions for cooking, then creaming, the potatoes given in Menu 7. If the cooked potatoes are sieved before adding the butter or margarine and milk, they will be perfectly free from lumps and could be piped around the edge of the dish with the Beef Olives.

   In this recipe it is quite satisfactory to add milk to the potatoes (see comments under Duchesse Potatoes in Menu 49) as the vegetable is not browned in the oven.

Macedoine of Vegetables

Peel the root vegetables, cut into 0.5cm (¼in) dice; prepare and dice the beans. Cook in boiling salted water until nearly tender, then add the peas and continue cooking for 5-6 minutes. Potatoes could be included in the Macedoine of Vegetables which would avoid the necessity of preparing Creamed Potatoes. Spoon some of the mixed vegetables around the Beef Olives; serve the rest separately.

Apricot Coconut Streusel

Put the apricots into a 1.2 litre (2pt) pie or oven-proof dish; arrange in as flat a layer as possible. Sprinkle the sugar over the fruit. Blend the lemon rind, lemon juice and water; spoon over the fruit. If the fruit is firm, cover the dish and bake for 15 minutes before adding the topping. Sift the flour and spice. Rub in the butter or margarine, add the sugar and the coconut. Sprinkle on top of the fruit. Flatten with the back of a metal spoon. Bake in the centre of a very moderate oven for 35-40 minutes until golden brown. Reduce heat slightly after 25 minutes if it becomes too brown. Serve hot with cream.

To Make Sunday Easier

1   Make Lofoten Caviar one or two days ahead; add egg garnish just before serving. Cover the cod's roe mixture to prevent drying.
2   Cook Beef Olives and reheat on Sunday; make sure the gravy and meat in the dish reach boiling point to ensure no harmful bacteria can develop. The Macedoine of Vegetables could be partially cooked.
3   Prepare and lightly cook apricots if required (see recipe); prepare topping but put over fruit just before cooking.

Foods Required

4 large slices topside of beef, 450g (1lb) uncooked cod's roe, 100-125g (4-5oz) butter or margarine plus butter for toast, 50g (2oz) fat or beef dripping, 50g (2oz) shredded suet, 3 eggs, 2-3tbspn milk, 300ml (½pt) cream, 200g (7oz) flour, 75g (3oz) sugar plus 1tspn, 100g (4oz) light brown sugar, 50g (2oz) desiccated coconut, 2-4tbspn oil, mixed spice, bread for toast and to give 100g (4oz) breadcrumbs, 450-675g (1-1½lb) old potatoes, ingredients for Macedoine of Vegetables (see recipe), 1 garlic clove or garlic salt, 1 bay leaf, parsley, fresh or dried thyme, 2 lemons, 450-675g (1-1½lb) fresh apricots.

Macedoine of Vegetables

Include carrots, turnips, swede, celeriac (if available), with beans and peas (you need approximately 675g (1½lb).

Apricot Coconut Streusel

450-675g (1-1½lb) fresh
  apricots
75g (3oz) sugar
¼tspn grated lemon rind
1-2tbspn lemon juice
2tbspn water

For the topping
175g (6oz) self-raising or plain
  flour
½tspn mixed spice
75g (3oz) butter or margarine
100g (4oz) light brown sugar
50g (2oz) desiccated coconut

Variations
1 Apricot Crumble: omit the coconut and mixed spice.
2 Use other fruit instead of apricots.

To Freeze Ahead

Lofoten Caviar: freeze for 2-3 weeks only; do not freeze hard-boiled egg garnish.
Beef Olives, like most casseroles, freezes well for up to 3 months. Do not over-cook the meat as reheating obviously continues the cooking process.
Macedoine of Vegetables: it is better to blanch uncooked vegetables, then freeze and cook. If cooked and frozen they tend to be over-soft.
Apricot Coconut Streusel: prepare and freeze (apricots are better if lightly cooked before freezing). Reheat as soon as defrosted to prevent topping becoming too soft. You can freeze the lightly cooked apricots in one container and the topping separately.

Cheese is a difficult flavour with which to 'match' a wine. Either serve a very well-chilled white wine or cold lager.

Waldorf Salad
4 small dessert apples
4tbspn French Dressing (see Menu 34)
small head celery
75g (3oz) walnuts
2tbspn mayonnaise (see Menu 34)
lettuce

Cheese Fondue
225g (8oz) Gruyère cheese
225g (8oz) Emmenthal cheese
7g (¼oz) butter
1 garlic clove
150ml (¼pt) dry white wine or cider
1-2tbspn brandy (optional)
salt and pepper
French bread or ordinary bread

Variations
1 Blend 1tspn cornflour with the wine to help prevent curdling.
2 Use Cheddar cheese.

Pineapple Coconut Cream
2 eggs
40g (1½oz) caster sugar
few drops vanilla essence
300ml (½pt) milk
2tspn gelatine
3tbspn pineapple syrup from can
75g (3oz) desiccated coconut
5-6 canned pineapple rings
150ml (¼pt) double cream

To Freeze Ahead
Pineapple Coconut Cream: allow to set, then freeze.

Menu 46	Waldorf Salad
Serves 4	Cheese Fondue
	Pineapple Coconut Cream

Waldorf Salad
Peel and dice the apples; put into the dressing at once so they keep a good colour. Cut the celery into neat pieces; chop the walnuts. Blend the celery, 50g (2oz) walnuts and mayonnaise (see Menu 34) with the apples and dressing. Shred the lettuce and put into a salad bowl; top with the apple mixture and the remaining walnuts.

Cheese Fondue
Grate the cheeses, rub the ceramic fondue pan with the butter. Halve the garlic clove and rub around the pan; if you do this after spreading with butter, the flavour lingers longer. Put the cheeses and wine or cider into the pan. You can start to heat the mixture on an ordinary cooker, stirring from time to time, until the cheese starts to melt, then transfer it to a proper fondue heater and leave until melted; adjust the heat so the mixture keeps hot without over-heating. If it does become too hot, it may curdle. Add the brandy and adjust the seasoning.

Cut French bread into small pieces or toast ordinary bread and then cut it into squares. Each person spears the bread or toast on a fondue fork and dips it into the hot creamy cheese mixture.

Pineapple Coconut Cream
Separate the eggs; beat together the yolks, sugar and vanilla essence; add the milk. Cook over a pan of hot water until a thickened custard. Sprinkle the gelatine on the pineapple syrup, stand over hot water until dissolved, blend with the warm custard, add the coconut. Allow to cool. Chop the pineapple, add to the gelatine mixture. Allow to stiffen slightly. Whip the cream until it holds its shape, and whisk the egg whites until stiff. Fold half the cream into the pineapple mixture, then the egg whites. Spoon into glasses. When firm, top with the remaining cream.

To Make Sunday Easier
1 Prepare salad ingredients; put in refrigerator. Make dressing.
2 Grate cheeses for the fondue. Place heater in a safe position.
3 Make the Pineapple Coconut Cream.

Foods Required
15g (½oz) butter, 225g (8oz) Gruyère cheese, 225g (8oz) Emmenthal cheese, 150ml (¼pt) double cream, 2 eggs, 300ml (½pt) milk, 40g (1½oz) caster sugar, generous amount of French or ordinary bread, 75g (3oz) desiccated coconut, 75g (3oz) walnuts, small can pineapple rings, vanilla essence, 2tspn gelatine, ingredients for French Dressing (see Menu 34), 2tbspn mayonnaise (see Menu 34), 150ml (¼pt) dry white wine or cider, 1-2tbspn brandy (optional), head celery, lettuce, 1 garlic clove, 4 dessert apples.

Menu 13
Lemon and Apricot Cheesecake

With this traditional joint of lamb serve a good full-bodied red Burgundy or Bordeaux or one of the red wines from Spain or Italy.

Melon Boats

1 good-sized honeydew melon
6 oranges slices
6 glacé cherries

Variations
Serve with slices of Parma or other smoked ham or with peeled prawns and light mayonnaise.

Stuffed Loin of Lamb

1.8kg (4lb) loin of lamb

For the stuffing
2 onions
225g (8oz) celery heart
50g (2oz) butter or margarine
100g (4oz) soft breadcrumbs
1tbspn chopped celery leaves
1tspn chopped fresh or ½tspn dried rosemary
1tbspn chopped parsley
2 egg yolks
1tbspn lemon juice
1tspn grated lemon rind
salt and pepper

Braised Celery

1 large head of celery
40g (1½oz) butter or margarine
40g (1½oz) flour
450ml (¾pt) lamb stock
scant 1tbspn tomato purée
salt and pepper

To garnish
chopped parsley

Variations
1 Cut celery into larger portions.
2 While one can 'echo' the celery flavouring of the stuffing, you may like to substitute whole leeks or onions instead.

Broccoli

approximately 675g (1½lb) broccoli
little salt
25g (1oz) butter

Menu 47   Melon Boats

Serves 6

Stuffed Loin of Lamb
Duchesse Potatoes
Braised Celery—Broccoli

Peach and Grape Vacherin

Melon Boats

Divide the melon into 6 portions, remove seeds. Slice the melon flesh so it is easy to eat, but keep on the skin. Put the orange slices and cherries on to cocktail sticks, press into the melon slices. Serve with sugar and ground ginger.

Stuffed Loin of Lamb

Bone the lamb, or ask the butcher to do it for you. Save the bones to make stock for the Braised Celery. Simmer these for 1 hour in water to cover, season lightly.

Peel and chop the onions; chop the celery finely. Heat the butter or margarine in a pan, fry the onions until tender, do not brown. Blend with the remaining ingredients. Flatten the meat, spread with the stuffing, roll or tie with string or secure with skewers to make a neat roll. Place in the roasting tin and cook as the table on page 10. If you use Temperature 2 (lower heat), the celery can be cooked in a covered dish in the oven.

For Duchesse Potatoes, see Menu 49.

Braised Celery

The advantage of including a braised vegetable in this menu, based upon roast meat, is that the gravy is already prepared and cooked with the celery, that is why a fairly high percentage of sauce is made. Cut the washed celery into 5cm (2in) pieces; discard tough part of stalks; any celery left from preparing the stuffing also could be used. Heat the butter or margarine in a pan, add the celery and fry gently for several minutes; lift the celery from the pan. Blend the flour with any fat remaining in the pan, stir in the stock, tomato purée, a little salt and pepper. Bring to the boil, stir until slightly thickened. The sauce may appear thick at this stage, but celery is a watery vegetable and it will become thinner. Either put the celery and sauce into a casserole and cook for 1 hour in the centre of a moderate oven, 180°C, 350°F, Gas Mark 4, or return the celery to the saucepan; cover this tightly and cook for 45 minutes over a low heat. Spoon the celery from the sauce, top with parsley. Adjust the consistency of the sauce by adding a little more liquid or by boiling hard to make it a little thicker; strain into sauce boat.

Broccoli

Trim the ends of the stalks of the broccoli; remove any tough outer leaves. It is not easy to give exactly the right weight for this vegetable since it varies so much. At some times of the year there is a lot of stalk and outer leaves, but little flower, which means you need to buy a greater amount.

Choose a really large saucepan, so you do not have too great a depth of this vegetable. Put enough cold water into the pan to give a depth of 3.5cm (1½in), bring to the boil. Add a little salt, then put in the broccoli. Cover the pan. Cook until tender; this can be from 5 minutes onwards since very young broccoli becomes tender very quickly. The water should boil fairly rapidly. Remove the vegetable from the pan very carefully; put into hot dish and top with the butter.

Peach and Grape Vacherin

Cut two 20cm (8in) rounds of greaseproof paper, place on to one or two baking trays; brush the paper with a few drops of olive oil or melted butter. You can, however, buy special 'non-stick' (silicone) paper which does not need greasing. Whisk the egg whites until very stiff; do not allow them to become dry and crumbly. Whisk in half the sugar, then fold in the remainder, together with the vanilla essence. Spoon the meringue mixture on to the rounds of paper; spread flat with a palette knife. Bake for about 2-3 hours in a very cool oven, 110°C, 225°F, Gas Mark ¼, until dry and crisp. Peel the paper from the meringues or remove from the trays while just warm. Allow to cool.

Whip the cream, fold in the sugar and vanilla essence. Drain the peaches (use the syrup for a fruit salad later in the week). Chop about half for the filling. Deseed, but do not skin the grapes; halve some for the filling. Spread half the cream over one round of meringue, top with the chopped peaches and half the grapes. Put the second round of meringue on top, spread with a little cream (save some for decoration). Top with the sliced peaches and grapes. Pipe a border of cream around the edge of the meringue.

To Make Sunday Easier

1 Prepare the stuffing, add to meat; secure as recipe. Make stock.
2 Cook potatoes; prepare Duchesse Potatoes if not being frozen (see Menu 49).
3 Lightly cook Braised Celery; reheat on Sunday or prepare dish ready to cook in the oven.
4 Bake meringue rounds if not done beforehand; if preparing Saturday, you can use the left-over whites (egg yolks used in stuffing and Duchesse Potatoes).

Foods Required

1.8kg (4lb) loin of lamb, 165-190g (6½-7½oz) butter or margarine, olive oil (optional), 300ml (½pt) double cream, 4-5 eggs (4 whites, 4-5 yolks), 40g (1½oz) flour, 225g (8oz) sugar either all caster or half caster and half icing sugar plus little extra, bread to give 100g (4oz) breadcrumbs, 1tbspn tomato purée, vanilla essence, ground ginger, 6 glacé cherries, large can peach slices, 2 onions, 1 large head celery and 1 celery heart to include few leaves, approximately 675g (1½lb) broccoli, 675-900g (1½-2lb) potatoes, fresh or dried rosemary, parsley, 1 good-sized honeydew melon, 1 lemon, 1 orange, 100g (4oz) white grapes, 100g (4oz) black grapes.

Variation

Broccoli with Hollandaise Sauce

Put 50-100g (2-4oz) butter at room temperature to soften. Put 2 egg yolks, salt, pepper and 1tbspn lemon juice or white wine vinegar into a basin over a pan of hot, but not boiling, water. Whisk until thick and creamy, then gradually whisk in the butter.

Peach and Grape Vacherin

For the meringue
4 egg whites
225g (8oz) sugar, either all caster sugar or half caster and half sieved icing sugar
few drops vanilla essence

For the filling and topping
300ml (½pt) double cream
1tbspn caster sugar
few drops vanilla essence
large can peach slices
100g (4oz) white grapes
100g (4oz) black grapes

Variations
1 The meringue can be given a slightly different texture, as in a traditional Pavlova, by folding in 1tspn white or brown malt vinegar to the whisked egg whites and adding 1tspn cornflour to the sugar.
2 Use other fresh or canned fruits.

To Freeze Ahead

Stuffed Loin of Lamb: this particular stuffing is not good when frozen, but lamb freezes well for up to 8 months. Duchesse Potatoes can be frozen. Cook without defrosting (see Menu 49).
Braised Celery can be frozen; use within 1 month.

A well-chilled dry sherry would blend well with the hors d'oeuvre. Follow this with chilled beer or a red wine.

Savoury Ramekins

100g (4oz) mushrooms
1 small red pepper
75g (3oz) butter
1tbspn chopped parsley
6 eggs
50g (2oz) finely grated hard
   cheese
salt and pepper

Variation
Add a few peeled prawns or diced smoked salmon to the mushrooms. You can omit any ingredients not enjoyed by children.

Steak and Kidney Pie

For the flaky pastry★
175g (6oz) plain flour
pinch salt
120g (4½oz) butter or use half
   butter or margarine and half
   lard
squeeze of lemon juice
water to bind

For the filling
550g (1¼lb) stewing steak
100-175g (4-6oz) ox kidney
20g (¾oz) flour
salt and pepper
50g (2oz) beef dripping or fat
450ml (¾pt) beef stock or
   water
1 large onion (optional)

To glaze
1 egg

Variations
1 Add 50-100g (2-4oz) button mushrooms to the meat mixture when putting into the pie dish; these would not be suitable in this menu as mushrooms are in the first course.
2 Slice 1 or 2 onions, fry with the meat.
3 Use shortcrust pastry made with 175-200g (6-7oz) flour, etc (see Menu 26).

Menu 48	Savoury Ramekins
Serves 4	Steak and Kidney Pie
	Roast Potatoes — Leeks
	Pears Rosamund

Savoury Ramekins

Wipe and slice the mushrooms. Wipe and dice the pepper; discard the core and seeds. Divide the butter between 4 small ramekin dishes. Heat for a few minutes towards the top of a moderately hot oven, 200°C, 400°F, Gas Mark 6. Divide the mushrooms and pepper between the dishes. Cook for 5 minutes. Blend the parsley, eggs and cheese with a little salt and pepper. Spoon into the dishes. Bake for 8 minutes or until just set. Serve with a teaspoon.

Steak and Kidney Pie

★The proportions given are sufficient for the pie in this menu. The classic proportions for flaky pastry are two-thirds fat to flour, so you would use 175g (6oz) fat to 225g (8oz) plain flour.

Sift the flour and salt into a mixing bowl. Soften the butter slightly with a knife, make into a neat oblong, then divide into 3 portions; if using a mixture of butter or margarine and lard, blend these together, form into a neat oblong; proceed as for butter. Rub in one-third of the butter or fats, add lemon juice and water to make an elastic dough. Roll out on a lightly floured board until a neat oblong; cut half the remaining butter or fats into small pieces, dot over two-thirds of the dough, leave the bottom part uncovered. Fold this lower third over the centre part; bring the top portion down to enclose the butter or fats between the layers. Give the dough a quarter turn to the right so the open end is towards you. Seal both ends with the rolling pin; 'rib' (depress the pastry at intervals) with the rolling pin to equalise the pressure of air.

Roll the dough out carefully to a rectangle again and repeat the above process with the remaining butter or fats. Turn, seal the ends and 'rib' the pastry. Wrap in foil or polythene, keep in the refrigerator while preparing the filling.

Cut the meat into 2.5cm (1in) cubes; discard the skin and tough parts of the kidney, cut into similar sized pieces as the beef. Blend the flour, salt and pepper on a plate, coat the meats in this; use all the flour. Heat the dripping or fat in a pan, fry the meats for about 5 minutes; blend in the stock or water, bring to the boil, stir over a low heat until slightly thickened. Peel the onion, add to the liquid if using this. Cover the pan, simmer gently for 2 hours or until the beef is just tender. Adjust the seasoning. Spoon the meat and a little gravy into a 1.2 litre (2pt) pie dish (see under A Good Pie, below); allow to cool. Remove the onion. Roll out the pastry thinly; cut a narrow strip and put this on the damp rim of the pie dish. Support the rest of the pastry over the rolling pin, place over the filling. Press the edges firmly together, cut away any surplus pastry with a sharp knife; flake the edges of the pastry and flute neatly. Make a slit on top of the pastry for steam to escape. Reroll any scraps of

102

pastry and cut out 'leaves' and a long strip for a pastry rose; moisten these with water, press on top of the pie. Beat the egg, brush over the pastry. Bake in the centre of a hot oven, 220°C, 425°F, Gas Mark 7, for 20-25 minutes, until the pastry has risen well, then lower the heat to moderate, 180-190°C, 350-375°F, Gas Mark 4-5, for a further 10-15 minutes. Heat the remaining gravy, add a little extra liquid if too stiff, then pour into a sauce boat.

Roast Potatoes

Peel the potatoes; halve if large, try and keep the sizes consistent so the potatoes cook evenly. Keep in cold water until ready to cook. Heat the dripping or fat in a tin; dry the potatoes well, roll round in the hot fat until coated. Cook for about 30 minutes towards the top of a hot oven, then you can continue cooking in a moderate oven for about 30 minutes. You can, of course, cook the potatoes in a hot oven throughout the period when the cooking time could be slightly reduced. If the potatoes are well coated with fat, they do not need turning.

For method of cooking leeks, see Menu 41.

Pears Rosamund

Place the macaroons in a shallow serving dish. Spoon the pear syrup over the macaroons. Arrange a pear on each macaroon, with the core side uppermost. Spoon the apricot jam into each pear, top with half the almonds and spoon the hot Saboyan Sauce, made as below, over the stuffed pears. Leave until cold, then top with more flaked almonds.

Saboyan Sauce

Put the egg yolks and sugar into a basin, balance over a pan of hot, but not boiling, water. Whisk until thick and creamy. Gradually whisk in the white wine and rum. This sauce can be served hot or cold.

To Make Sunday Easier

1 Prepare mushroom and pepper mixture for Savoury Ramekins unless this is being frozen.
2 Make the pie unless it is being frozen. Cover uncooked pastry, put into refrigerator. This could be cooked the day beforehand and reheated without spoiling the flavour.

Foods Required

550g (1¼lb) stewing steak, 100-175g (4-6oz) ox kidney, 195g (7½oz) butter (unless using lard in pastry), 100g (4oz) fat unless using dripping, 50g (2oz) Cheddar or other hard cheese, 10 eggs (7 whites only used), 200g (7oz) plain flour, 75g (3oz) caster sugar, canned pears (8 halves needed plus 2tbspn syrup), 3tbspn apricot jam, 2tbspn blanched flaked almonds, 8 macaroon biscuits, 4tbspn white wine, 1tbspn rum, 100g (4oz) mushrooms, 1 small red pepper, 1 large onion (optional), 450-550g (1-1¼lb) potatoes, 8 medium leeks, parsley, 1 lemon (squeeze of juice only required).

Roast Potatoes

450-550g (1-1¼lb) potatoes
50g (2oz) clarified dripping or
   fat

Variation
Par-boil the potatoes for 15 minutes in boiling salted water, drain, dry well and roast for about 35 minutes in a hot oven.

Leeks

8 medium leeks
salt

Pears Rosamund

8 macaroon biscuits
2tbspn canned pear syrup
8 halves canned pears
3tbspn apricot jam
2tbspn blanched flaked almonds

Saboyan Sauce

3 egg yolks★
75g (3oz) caster sugar
4tbspn white wine
1tbspn rum

★Use egg whites in meringues (see Menu 23).

To Freeze Ahead

Savoury Ramekins: freeze cooked mushroom and pepper mixture; do not freeze the complete dish.
Steak and Kidney Pie can be frozen for up to 3 months; do not over-cook meat as reheating helps to tenderise this.
Gravy can be frozen.

A Good Pie

Make sure the filling is high in the pie dish to prevent pastry 'falling in' during cooking. If your pie dish is a little large, as it may be for the pie in this menu and in Menu 7, use an egg cup or pie support with the filling. Remember, fruit sinks in cooking, so should be piled extra high.

As the gammon has a sweet flavour choose the new season's Beaujolais (lightly chilled) or a slightly sweet Italian Chianti or a light red Valpolicella.

Caesar Salad
2 eggs
2 large slices bread
50g (2oz) butter
1 garlic clove
100g (4oz) Cheddar cheese
1 lettuce
3 tomatoes
¼ medium cucumber
5tbspn mayonnaise (see Menu 34)
1 can anchovy fillets

Honey Glazed Gammon
1.8-2.25kg (4-5lb) gammon in one piece
2 medium onions (optional)
2 medium carrots (optional)
shake black pepper or 6 peppercorns
1 bay leaf

For the glaze
3tbspn clear honey
1tspn ground cinnamon
1tspn mustard powder
2tbspn Demerara sugar

To garnish
6-8 canned pineapple rings
watercress

Variation
Use less expensive forehock or collar and cook for 35-40 minutes per 450g (1lb).

Mustard Sauce
40g (1½oz) butter or margarine
40g (1½oz) flour
1tspn mustard powder
300ml (½pt) milk
300ml (½pt) bacon stock
1tbspn chopped parsley
salt and pepper

Duchesse Potatoes
675-900g (1½-2lb) old potatoes
salt and pepper
50-75g (2-3oz) butter
2-3 egg yolks (use whites in soufflé in this menu)

Menu 49

Serves 6

Caesar Salad

Honey Glazed Gammon with Mustard Sauce
Duchesse Potato Nests with Peas
Carrots and Onions

Coffee Soufflé with Chocolate Sauce

Caesar Salad
Hard-boil the eggs. Cut the bread into small dice. Heat the butter in a frying pan; fry the bread until crisp and golden on both sides; drain on absorbent paper. Peel the garlic clove, halve and rub round the inside of a salad bowl. Grate the cheese. Prepare the lettuce, shred and put into the bowl. Slice the tomatoes and cucumber; shell and slice the eggs, add to the bowl; top with the mayonnaise, grated cheese and the well-drained anchovy fillets. Tip the croûtons on top of the salad just before serving.

Honey Glazed Gammon
Soak well salted gammon in cold water to cover for 12 hours. Mildly cured gammon ('green' or sweet-cure) does not require soaking. Peel the onions and carrots, leave whole. Put the gammon, vegetables, pepper or peppercorns and the bay leaf into a saucepan; cover with fresh water. Bring to simmering point, lower the heat, cover the pan and cook steadily. Allow 20-25 minutes per 450g (1lb) and 20-25 minutes over. A thinner and wider cut is generally tender in the shorter time. Remove the gammon from the liquid, drain well, cut away the skin, score the fat. Lift into a roasting tin.

Blend the ingredients for the glaze; spread over the fat. Cook for 20 minutes above the centre of a moderate oven, 180-190°C, 350-375°F, Gas Mark 4-5, or until golden brown. Garnish with the pineapple rings and watercress. Use left-over pineapple syrup in a fruit salad.

Mustard Sauce
Heat the butter or margarine in a saucepan. Stir in the flour and mustard. Blend in the milk and stock, stir until boiling, then continue stirring over a low heat until slightly thickened; this sauce should not be too thick. Stir in the remaining ingredients.

Duchesse Potatoes
Cook the potatoes in boiling salted water, strain, then sieve. Return to the saucepan, warm gently; beat in the butter, then the egg yolks. Season well. Do not add milk, for the potatoes would lose their shape when heated. Put a 1-2.5cm (½-1in) rose into a large piping bag. Pipe the warm potato mixture in attractive shapes on a greased baking tray or oven-proof serving dish. Place in the oven until well heated and brown. The timing depends upon the actual menu; this menu takes about 15 minutes.
Duchesse Potato Nests with Peas Pipe in neat small flan shapes; brown and fill with cooked peas.

Carrots and Onions

Peel the vegetables; leave whole and cook in well-strained gammon stock. They can be cooked in boiling salted water.

Coffee Soufflé

Blend the cornflour with the milk and coffee. Put into a large saucepan, add the butter, sugar and cream. Stir over a low heat until a thick sauce. Separate the 3 eggs. Remove the pan from the heat, beat in the egg yolks. Whisk the 6 egg whites until they stand in peaks; fold into the coffee mixture, then spoon into a lightly buttered 18-20cm (7-8in) soufflé dish. Sweet soufflés can be baked successfully in wider and more shallow dishes. Bake in the centre of a moderate oven, 180-190°C, 350-375°F, Gas Mark 4-5, for about 35 minutes until well risen and firm on top. Allow about 25 minutes for a shallow dish. These times produce a soufflé with a slightly soft centre. Sift the icing sugar over the top and serve at once.
Note The mixture can be prepared up to 1 hour before the meal. Spoon into the prepared dish and *cover completely* with an upturned mixing bowl to exclude all air.

Chocolate Sauce

The sauce is not essential but it makes a more elaborate dessert.

Break the chocolate in pieces. Put in a basin, add the other ingredients and melt over hot, but not boiling, water or in a microwave cooker. Keep warm until ready to serve over the water.
Note Never allow the mixture to become over-heated as this causes the chocolate to lose its gloss.

To Make Sunday Easier

1 Fry Croûtons for salad if these are not frozen; grate cheese, put in covered container in the refrigerator.
2 The gammon could be cooked on Saturday, kept in the liquid, then glazed and heated on Sunday. If following this procedure, you will need to heat for about 35-40 minutes at a slightly lower temperature than the one given in the recipe.
3 Cook and pipe Duchesse Potatoes on to an oven-proof serving dish or greased baking tray; keep in the refrigerator.

Foods Required

1.8-2.25kg (4-5lb) gammon in one piece (buy in plenty of time if it needs soaking), 195-220g (7½-8½oz) butter, 100g (4oz) Cheddar cheese, 4tbspn double cream, 8 eggs, nearly 600ml (1pt) milk unless using single cream in Chocolate Sauce, 175g (6oz) plain chocolate, 40g (1½oz) flour, 100g (4oz) caster sugar, 25g (1oz) icing sugar, 2tbspn Demerara sugar, bread to give 2 slices, 5tbspn mayonnaise (see Menu 34), 2tbspn cornflour, 1 can anchovy fillets, 6-8 rings canned pineapple, 3 tbspn clear honey, ground cinnamon, mustard, black pepper or 6 peppercorns, coffee, 675-900g (1½-2lb) old potatoes, lettuce, 3 tomatoes, ¼ medium cucumber, 450g (1lb) small onions plus 2 medium ones (optional), 450g (1lb) small carrots plus 2 medium ones (optional), watercress, parsley, bay leaf, 1 garlic clove.

Duchesse Potato Nests with Peas

ingredients as above
approximately 175g (6oz)
  frozen peas

Carrots and Onions

450g (1lb) small carrots
450g (1lb) small onions
salt and pepper

Coffee Soufflé

2tbspn cornflour
150ml (¼pt) milk
150ml (¼pt) very strong coffee
40g (1½oz) butter
75g (3oz) caster sugar
4tbspn double cream
3 eggs
3 egg whites (yolks used in
  Duchesse Potato Nests)
25g (1oz) icing sugar

Chocolate Sauce

175g (6oz) plain chocolate
25g (1oz) caster sugar
6tbspn milk or single cream
15g (½oz) butter

Variation
Mocha Sauce: use half very strong coffee and half single cream.

To Freeze Ahead

Caesar Salad: fry croûtons, spread flat on absorbent paper on a flat baking tray; open-freeze, then put into a container. The crisp dice should be defrosted for the salad; if by any chance they seem a little soft, crisp in the oven for 4-5 minutes, then cool.
Duchesse Potato Nests can be piped on to a greased baking tray or oven-proof dish, frozen and then covered. Reheat from the frozen state, then fill with the cooked peas.

Although this menu is planned to extend expensive meat, it is still a meal that justifies the best red wine.

Citrus Sorbet
300ml (½pt) water
75g (3oz) sugar
2tspn gelatine
300ml (½pt) orange juice
2tbspn lemon juice
3tbspn grapefruit juice
3 egg whites
12 orange segments

Steaks en Croûte with Tomatoes
puff pastry made with 175g (6oz) plain flour, 175g (6oz) butter (see Menu 9)
6 small fillet steaks
2 medium onions
100g (4oz) mushrooms
25g (1oz) butter
2tbspn chopped parsley
salt and pepper
1 egg
6 large tomatoes

Potato Croquettes
675g (1½lb) old potatoes
salt and pepper
50g (2oz) butter
25g (1oz) flour
1 egg
50g (2oz) crisp breadcrumbs

To fry
oil

Caramel Custard
200g (7oz) sugar
5tbspn water
4 eggs
3 egg yolks
300ml (½pt) double cream
900ml (1½pt) milk

To Freeze Ahead
Sorbet freezes well for weeks.
Steaks en Croûte: freeze puff pastry, but not the prepared dish.
Potato Croquettes: open-freeze, then pack.

Menu 50

Citrus Sorbet

Serves 6

Steak en Croûte with Tomatoes
Potato Croquettes—Green Salad

Caramel Custard

Citrus Sorbet
Heat the water and sugar, add the gelatine and stir until dissolved. Cool, mix with the fruit juices. Freeze lightly, whisk the egg whites until very stiff, fold into the half-frozen mixture; continue freezing. Scoop in balls into glasses; garnish with orange segments.

Steaks en Croûte with Tomatoes
Prepare the pastry; grill the steaks to personal taste, but remove from the heat before quite cooked. Peel and finely chop the onions, chop the mushrooms. Heat the butter, fry the vegetables until soft, add the parsley and seasoning; top steaks with this mixture, then cool. Roll out pastry until wafer-thin; cut in 6 large squares. Place steaks on pastry and wrap this round the meat, seal joins firmly, glaze with beaten egg. Bake for 10 minutes in the centre of a very hot oven, 230°C, 450°F, Gas Mark 8, then for 15 minutes at a slightly lower heat.

Halve tomatoes, season, bake for 10 minutes.

Potato Croquettes
Cook potatoes in boiling salted water, strain, mash with butter. Form into finger shapes, coat in seasoned flour, then beaten egg and crisp breadcrumbs. Fry in hot oil or fat as described in Menu 30.

For Green Salad, see Menu 37.

Caramel Custard
Make a caramel as described in Menu 5, with 150g (5oz) sugar and the water, but keep it golden in colour. Pour into a 1.5 litre (2½pt) oven-proof mould or tin. Beat the eggs, egg yolks, remaining sugar, cream and milk. Strain over the caramel. Bake as in Menu 5, but allow about 2 hours until the custard is firm. Turn out when warm. Serve with cream.

To Make Sunday Easier
1   Freeze the sorbet when convenient.
2   Cook the steaks, topping; make the pastry; cook and coat croquettes.
3   Cook the Caramel Custard.

Foods Required
6 small fillet steaks, 250g (9oz) butter plus extra for cooking steaks, 300ml (½pt) double cream, 9 eggs, 900ml (1½pt) milk, 200g (7oz) plain flour, 275g (10oz) sugar, 50g (2oz) crisp breadcrumbs, 2tspn gelatine, 6 large tomatoes, 675g (1½lb) old potatoes, 2 medium onions, 100g (4oz) mushrooms, ingredients for Green Salad (see Menu 37), and French Dressing (see Menu 34), 300ml (½pt) orange juice, 2-3 oranges, 2tbspn lemon juice, 3tbspn grapefruit juice, parsley.

Menu 49
Honey Glazed Gammon with Mustard Sauce, Duchesse Potato Nests with Peas, Carrots and Onions

A fine red Bordeaux (claret) would be an ideal accompaniment, but these are expensive so try good Rhône or Spanish wines.

Prawn and Apple Cocktail

1tbspn lemon juice
3tbspn mayonnaise (Menu 34)
3tbspn yoghurt
salt and pepper
2 red-skinned dessert apples
100g (4oz) peeled prawns
lettuce heart

Variation
Omit the apples and add 100g (4oz) sliced raw button mushrooms.

Roast Pheasant

1 large young pheasant or 2 smaller birds (the cock bird is larger but hen pheasant plump). If buying 2 pheasants you generally have 'a brace', ie a cock and a hen.
100-150g (4-5oz) butter or use 50-65g (2-2½oz) butter for stuffing the bird(s) and a few bacon rashers for covering the bird(s)

Variation
Use cream cheese instead of butter, or cream cheese plus a few skinned and deseeded grapes.

Port Wine Sauce

For the stock
giblets of pheasant(s)
1 small onion
1 bay leaf
salt and pepper

For the sauce
25g (1oz) butter
25g (1oz) flour
300ml (½pt) pheasant stock
3tbspn port wine
1tbspn redcurrant jelly

Variation
Use strained fat from cooking the pheasant(s) instead of butter.

Menu 51	Prawn and Apple Cocktail
Serves 4	Roast Pheasant with Port Wine Sauce or Gravy
	Redcurrant Jelly or Bread Sauce
	Game Chips—Fried Crumbs
	Potatoes Anna—Brussels Sprouts
	Meringue Ice-cream

Prawn and Apple Cocktail

Blend together the lemon juice, mayonnaise, yoghurt and a little salt and pepper. Core, but do not peel, the apples, then cut into very small dice. Place in the dressing; stand for about 15 minutes. Add the prawns. Shred the lettuce very finely, put into 4 glasses or on small plates. Top with the prawn and apple mixture.

This makes a pleasant change from the more usual Prawn Cocktail with a Mary Rose (tomato-flavoured) Dressing, used in Menu 9.

Roast Pheasant

Pheasants are surprisingly meaty game birds. If the family has small appetites, one plump pheasant is just about enough for 4 servings. Cold pheasant is delicious, so 2 pheasants would ensure generous portions and there would be a little meat left over. The giblets should be simmered for gravy or the Port Wine Sauce (see recipe below). Any stock left over is splendid for the basis for soup.

Pheasants are a lean bird, inclined to dry if not kept moist during cooking. Although a stuffing can be put inside the bird, as for chicken or turkey, this is not usual. A knob of butter will, however, make sure the bird is kept moist. Put half the butter into the body of the bird(s); the smaller amount is enough for one bird. Spread the rest of the butter over the outside of the bird, or use bacon rashers instead. Weigh and roast as shown in the table on page 10. When serving roast pheasant you can adorn the dish with the tail feathers if desired.

Serve with redcurrant jelly or Bread Sauce (see Menu 52).

Port Wine Sauce

Put the giblets of the pheasant in water to cover; check there is no green mark of a broken gall bladder on the liver for this gives a very bitter taste to the stock. Peel the onion, add to the water with a bay leaf, salt and pepper. Simmer for about 45 minutes, then strain the stock. Put 300ml (½pt) on one side. Heat the butter in a pan, stir in the flour, cook for 2-3 minutes, then gradually blend in the stock; stir as the sauce comes to the boil, then continue stirring as it thickens. Add the port wine, redcurrant jelly and a little seasoning.

Game Chips

Peel the potatoes and cut into wafer-thin slices; the slicing attachment on a mixer or food processor is ideal for this purpose. Keep in cold water until ready to cook, then dry very thoroughly.

Heat the pan of deep oil or fat; put in the frying basket to heat at the same time so the potatoes do not stick to this. The fat can be heated to 190°C, 375°F, as the potatoes are so thin. This means a cube of day-old bread turns golden within less than 30 seconds. Put in the potatoes and fry for 2-3 minutes or until crisp and brown. Drain on absorbent paper. The potatoes can be fried ahead, put on to a flat tray or dish and reheated in the oven. It is worthwhile frying quite a batch of these and storing left-over potatoes for another occasion. To serve, place around the pheasant or in a separate dish.

Fried Crumbs

Heat the butter or fat in a large frying pan. Add the crumbs, turn in the butter or fat until evenly coated, then continue cooking until crisp and golden brown. Drain on absorbent paper. These can be fried earlier, spread on a flat dish and put into the oven for just a few minutes to reheat. They burn easily so do not leave in the oven for too long a period. Serve in a small dish or sauce boat.

For Potatoes Anna see Menu 28; Brussels Sprouts see Menu 6.

Meringue Ice-cream

Brown the almonds under the grill or in the oven; quarter the cherries. Put the sultanas into a basin, add the orange juice and allow to stand for 1 hour. Allow the ice-cream to soften slightly. Blend most of the almonds, cherries and moistened sultanas with the ice-cream. Freeze for a short time so that it is not too soft. Break 3 meringues into 4-6 pieces. Fold half the pieces into the ice-cream. Return to the freezer until ready to serve. Crush the remaining meringue. Top each portion of ice-cream with the meringue crumbs and remaining almonds, cherries and sultanas.

To Make Sunday Easier

1 Prepare Port Wine Sauce or simmer pheasant giblets to make stock for gravy.
2 Cook Game Chips and Fried Crumbs; reheat as in recipe.
3 Make and freeze Meringue Ice-cream.

Foods Required

1 large young pheasant or 2 smaller birds, 100g (4oz) peeled prawns, 225-275g (9-10oz) butter or 175-190g (7-7½oz) butter and few streaky bacon rashers, 2 large eggs, 300ml (½pt) whipping or double cream, 3tbspn yoghurt, 25g (1oz) flour, 50g (2oz) icing sugar, ingredients for Bread Sauce (see Menu 52) make half quantity, ingredients for meringues (3 needed) (see Menu 23), 3tbspn mayonnaise (see Menu 34), 3tbspn port wine if not serving gravy, 1tbspn redcurrant jelly plus extra if not serving Bread Sauce, oil or fat for frying, bread to give 75g (3oz) breadcrumbs, 25g (1oz) flaked blanched almonds, 50g (2oz) glacé or Maraschino cherries, 50g (2oz) sultanas, 2tbspn orange juice, vanilla essence, 1 small onion, 450g (1lb) old potatoes plus 2-3 large ones, 1 bay leaf, 450g (1lb) Brussels sprouts, lettuce, 2 red-skinned dessert apples, 1 lemon.

Game Chips

2-3 large old potatoes

For frying

oil or fat

Variation
Buy potato crisps, spread on a flat tray, heat in the oven.

Fried Crumbs

50g (2oz) butter or fat
75g (3oz) coarse soft bread-crumbs

Meringue Ice-cream

25g (1oz) flaked blanched almonds
50g (2oz) glacé or Maraschino cherries
50g (2oz) sultanas
2tbspn orange juice
ice-cream (see Menu 18)
4 meringue shells (Menu 23)

Variation
Use commercial ice-cream.

To Freeze Ahead

Bread Sauce: freeze with onion in sauce.
Fried Crumbs: open-freeze on flat baking tray padded with absorbent paper; when frozen, pack into polythene box.
Potatoes Anna freezes quite well, although the potatoes lose some of their texture.
Meringue Ice-cream: in either the freezing compartment of a refrigerator or in the freezer.

Home-made Mayonnaise

Mayonnaise as used in the hors d'oeuvre in this menu and other dishes can be made by hand or with a liquidiser or food processor (Menu 22).

Make sure egg yolks and oil are at room temperature.

To make the dressing by hand, beat 2 egg yolks with pinch salt, pepper, sugar, dry mustard powder. Whisk in up to 300ml (½pt) olive or salad oil to egg yolks drop by drop, then 1-2tbspn lemon juice or white wine vinegar.

Christmas is the time for special wines and food. You may like to be luxurious and serve champagne before or with the meal. For economy a sparkling Loire white wine or Spanish Freixenet (made by the champagne method) are good substitutes.

Virtually any wine can accompany turkey—you could choose a dry white wine or a good red Burgundy or claret. A sweet white wine or a Madeira is a good choice to serve with the pudding.

Grapefruit Baskets
4 good-sized grapefruit
small bunch white grapes
small bunch black grapes
sugar as desired

Variation
Sprinkle a little dry sherry over the fruit before chilling.

Roast Turkey
6-7kg (16-18lb) turkey
175g (6oz) butter

Sausages
675-900g (1½-2lb) pork sausages

Bacon Rolls
8-10 streaky bacon rashers

> # Menu 52
> *Serves 8*
>
> Grapefruit Baskets
>
> Roast Turkey with Sausages, Bacon Rolls and Gravy
> Chestnut Stuffing—Savoury Herb Stuffing
> Cranberry and Orange Sauce—Bread Sauce
> Roast Potatoes—Brussels Sprouts
> Braised Celery and/or Peas with Sweetcorn
>
> Christmas Pudding
> Brandy Butter—Sherry Custard Sauce
> Iced Christmas Pudding
> Mince Pies
>
> Cheese—Nuts—Fruit

Grapefruit Baskets
Halve the grapefruit, remove the segments of fruit and cut away any skin and pith left in the skins. Serrate the rims of the grapefruit skins with a pair of kitchen scissors. Deseed, but do not skin the grapes. Blend the grapefruit segments and grapes together. Spoon back into the grapefruit skins, sprinkle with a little sugar. Chill well.

Roast Turkey
Always defrost a frozen turkey thoroughly before roasting. Simmer the giblets (exclude the liver) for stock to make the gravy and use with the celery. Prepare the stuffings; put the Chestnut Stuffing inside the bird and the Savoury Herb Stuffing at the neck end. Brush the bird with melted butter. While you can roast turkey with the breast side uppermost, I find it is more moist if placed in the roasting tin with the breast downwards and cooked this way for the first half of the cooking period, then turned over, basted with the fat from the roasting tin and roasted with the breast uppermost for the remainder of the cooking period.

Always weigh the bird after stuffing and roast as the timing on page 10. If you are having Roast Potatoes, use Temperature 1. If you prefer to roast the bird more slowly you can substitute Duchesse Potatoes (see Menu 49) or boiled potatoes.

Sausages
Grease and pre-heat a separate tin and put in the sausages. Cook for 25-30 minutes at Temperature 1 (see page 10); these can be roasted around the turkey.

Bacon Rolls
Derind the bacon rashers, stretch with the back of a knife (this makes it easier to roll the bacon), halve and roll. The rolls can be secured with small wooden cocktail sticks or put on to long metal skewers, but if rolled firmly they should remain a good shape without skewers. Cook for about 15-20 minutes.

Menu 52
Roast Turkey with Sausages and Bacon Rolls, Roast Potatoes, Brussels Sprouts, Peas with Sweetcorn; Christmas Pudding; Mince Pies

Chestnut Stuffing

675g (1½lb) chestnuts
salt and pepper
2 medium onions
100g (4oz) mushrooms
75g (3oz) butter
4 bacon rashers (as fat as
  possible)
3-4 sticks celery, from the heart
3tbspn chopped parsley
1tspn chopped fresh or ½tspn
  dried thyme
225g (8oz) pork sausagemeat
1 egg
3tbspn tomato juice

Savoury Herb Stuffing

turkey liver
225g (8oz) soft breadcrumbs
100g (4oz) shredded suet
5tbspn chopped parsley
2tspn chopped fresh or 1tspn
  dried thyme
1tspn chopped fresh or ½tspn
  dried rosemary
2tspn finely grated lemon rind
3tbspn lemon juice
salt and pepper
garlic salt to taste
2 eggs or 4 egg yolks

Cranberry and Orange Sauce

150ml (¼pt) sweet white wine
  or water
2 large oranges
150g (5oz) sugar or to taste
3tbspn orange jelly marmalade
450g (1lb) cranberries

Variations
1 Use a little more or less
sugar if desired.
2 Use redcurrant jelly instead
of marmalade (jelly-type is
important).

Bread Sauce

1 medium onion
3-4 cloves (optional)
600ml (1pt) milk
100g (4oz) soft white breadcrumbs
50-75g (2-3oz) butter
salt and pepper
4-5tbspn double cream
  (optional)

Gravy

While there is an appreciable amount of sauce with the Braised Celery most people like extra gravy. Strain the giblet stock and make a good thickened gravy, as the recipe on page 10.

Chestnut Stuffing

There are many recipes for Chestnut Stuffing. This one is less usual and has a very definite flavour. If using fresh chestnuts, prepare and boil as in Menu 3. After skinning, simmer for 25 minutes in salted water. Peel and chop the onions, wipe and slice the mushrooms very thinly. Heat the butter in a pan and fry the onions and mushrooms for a few minutes. Derind and finely chop the bacon. Sieve the chestnuts or put into a liquidiser or food processor until a smooth purée. Chop the celery very finely. Blend together the chestnut purée and the rest of the ingredients.

Savoury Herb Stuffing

Chop the raw turkey liver. Blend with the rest of the ingredients.

Cranberry and Orange Sauce

Put the white wine or water into a saucepan. Grate the 'zest' from both oranges, put in the pan, cover and simmer for about 15 minutes. Lift the lid towards the end of this time so the liquid is reduced to about half. Add the sugar and marmalade to the liquid, stir over a low heat until dissolved. Put the cranberries into the pan, cover; they tend to explode during the first stages of cooking. Cook gently until the fruit is tender. Halve the oranges, remove the segments of fruit very carefully so they keep firm. Dice and add to the cranberry mixture. While this sauce can be served cold this version is very good hot.

Bread Sauce

Peel the onion; press the cloves into this. Put the onion into the milk, bring to the boil; add the breadcrumbs, butter, salt and pepper. Cover the pan, allow to stand for at least 1 hour in a warm place. You can, however, prepare the sauce in a covered casserole or dish in the oven. Just before lunch reheat the sauce if making in a saucepan. Remove the onion, beat in the cream and leave to heat for a few more minutes; adjust the seasoning.

Braised Celery

Prepare the celery as described in Menu 47; cut into neat portions (2 heads of celery will give generous portions). Continue as the recipe in Menu 47, but use turkey stock instead of lamb stock. Less sauce could be made as gravy is included in this Christmas menu.

Christmas Pudding

Blend all the ingredients together. Allow to stand overnight if possible; this seems to help the various foods to blend together. Stir well to mix; it is traditional for all the family to stir the mixture and make a wish. The basic amount given makes just about 1.5kg (3¼lb) in weight, so should be put into two basins of about 1.2 litres (2pt) capacity, each of which give good portions for 6 people or smaller portions for up to 8. A Christmas Pudding does not rise like a light pudding, but does swell in cooking so never overfill the basin(s). Grease the basin(s), put in the mixture, cover with greased greaseproof paper and foil or a cloth. Steam for 5-6 hours, remove damp covers, put on fresh dry covers at once. Store in a cool dry place. Resteam for 2 hours on Christmas Day. If steaming in one 2.4 litre (4pt) basin allow about 7 hours original steaming time and 3 hours on Christmas Day.

To ignite: stand the bottle of brandy or rum in a pan of hot water away from the cooker while enjoying main course. Pour a little over the hot pudding, light and carry into the dining-room.

Brandy Butter

Cream the butter until very soft. Sift the icing sugar and blend with the butter, beat again until a light mixture. Gradually beat in the brandy; do this slowly so the mixture does not curdle. Pipe or spoon into an attractive shape in a serving dish. Cut the cherries and angelica into tiny pieces and push into the butter mixture. Chill until firm; cover lightly with clingfilm.

Sherry Custard Sauce

Blend the custard powder and sugar with a little cold milk. Bring the rest of the milk to the boil, pour over the custard mixture. Return to the saucepan, stir over a low heat until thickened. Take out any of the custard required for young children, then blend the sherry into the remaining custard left in the saucepan.

Iced Christmas Pudding

Put the raisins and sultanas into a mixing bowl. Blend the peel and almonds. Halve the cherries, add to the fruit. Pour the sherry or orange juice over the dried fruit. Leave for several hours. Sift the icing sugar, add the eggs and whisk until a thick creamy mixture. Whisk the double cream, then whip in the single cream until the mixture stands in light peaks. Blend together the cream and whisked eggs. Freeze lightly, then gently fold in all the other ingredients (this method makes certain the fruits do not sink to the bottom of the container). Spoon into a 1.5 litre (2½-3pt) basin. Freeze until firm. Unmould and decorate with holly, like a true Christmas Pudding. Serve with cream.

Christmas Pudding

110g (4oz) of each of the following: flour, shredded suet or melted butter, soft breadcrumbs, moist brown sugar, chopped blanched almonds, chopped candied peel, grated raw cooking apple, currants, sultanas
225g (8oz) seedless raisins
50g (2oz) grated raw carrot
grated rind of 1 lemon and 1 orange
2tbspn lemon juice
1tspn mixed spice
1tspn ground cinnamon
½tspn grated nutmeg
2 large eggs
150ml (¼pt) stout
1tbspn black treacle or golden syrup

Variations
You can add 50-100g (2-4oz) of each of the following: chopped glacé cherries, chopped dried apricots, chopped dried prunes.

Brandy Butter

175g (6oz) unsalted butter
225g (8oz) icing sugar
3tbspn brandy

To decorate
glacé or Maraschino cherries
angelica

Sherry Custard Sauce

2tbspn custard powder
50-75g (2-3oz) sugar
900ml (1½pt) milk
2-3tbspn sweet sherry

Iced Christmas Pudding

110g (4oz) of each of the following: seedless raisins, sultanas, candied peel, chopped blanched almonds, glacé cherries
3tbspn sweet sherry or orange juice
75g (3oz) icing sugar
2 large eggs
150ml (¼pt) double cream
150ml (¼pt) single cream
25g (1oz) cocoa powder
2tspn black treacle
½tspn grated nutmeg

Mince Pies

For the mincemeat

110g (4oz) of each of the
following: shredded suet or
melted butter, grated raw
cooking apple, chopped
blanched almonds, chopped
candied peel, Demerara or
light brown sugar, currants,
sultanas

225g (8oz) seedless or chopped
raisins

grated rind of 1 lemon

2tbspn lemon juice

1tspn mixed spice

½tspn ground cinnamon

½tspn grated nutmeg

4tbspn brandy, whisky, rum or
orange juice

pastry (see method)

To Freeze Ahead

Turkey: if buying frozen
turkey, allow adequate time for
complete defrosting, ie up to
48 hours.
Chestnut Stuffing freezes for up
to 6 weeks.
Savoury Herb Stuffing freezes
for up to 3 months.
Cranberry and Orange Sauce
freezes for up to 6 months.
Bread Sauce freezes for up to 3
months.
Christmas Pudding does not
need freezing unless storage
conditions are poor. If freezing,
allow to defrost 1 week before
Christmas.
Brandy Butter: freeze for 1-2
weeks only, but there is a slight
loss of flavour.
Iced Christmas Pudding freezes
for up to 3 months.
Mince pies can be cooked and
frozen. Use within 3 months.

Mince Pies

Mix all the ingredients together. Put into dry jars, cover, store in a cool dry place. If using orange juice, the mincemeat should be stored in the refrigerator for several weeks or in the freezer.

Mince Pies can be made with shortcrust, sweet shortcrust or richer fleur pastry; you can use flaky or puff pastry. Recipes for these are indexed on page 119.

To make about 12 Mince Pies use pastry made with 225g (8oz) flour (or a little less with the richer pastries which have a higher percentage of fat). Roll out the pastry thinly. Cut half the rounds about 8cm (3in) for the base, half 6.5cm (2½in) for the top. Press into the patty tins. Spoon in a little mincemeat. Moisten the edges of the pastry. Put on the 'lids', press the edges of the pastry firmly together. Make 2 slits on top of the pastry for the steam to escape (use kitchen scissors). Bake in the centre of the oven. Use a moderately hot to hot oven, 200-220°C, 400-425°F, Gas Mark 6-7, for shortcrust pastry; moderately hot oven, 190-200°C, 375-400°F, Gas Mark 5-6, for fleur pastry, and a hot oven, 220°C, 425°F, Gas Mark 7, for the richer flaky or puff-pastry pies. Check after 10-15 minutes; if the pastry is becoming over-brown, lower the heat slightly. Top the Mince Pies with caster or icing sugar before serving.

To Prepare Ahead if Freezer Not Used

Some weeks ahead: make Christmas Pudding and mincemeat.
3-4 days ahead: make brandy butter; chill, then cover. Bake Mince Pies; store in airtight tin. Freeze Iced Christmas Pudding in freezing compartment of refrigerator.
2 days ahead: make stuffings and Cranberry and Orange Sauce.
Day before: prepare Grapefruit Baskets; cover and chill. Stuff turkey; simmer giblets. Make gravy, Braised Celery and Bread Sauce. Prepare vegetables.

Foods Required Just Before Christmas

6-7kg (16-18lb) turkey (including liver), 675-900g (1½-2lb) pork sausages, 175g (6oz) butter, approximately 100g (4oz) fat for roasting potatoes, selection of cheeses, 900ml (1½pt) milk, flour for gravy, 50-75g (2-3oz) sugar plus little extra, 8-10 streaky bacon rashers, 2tbspn custard powder, 2-3tbspn sweet sherry, brandy or rum to ignite pudding, 1-1.25kg (2-3lb) potatoes, 900g (2lb) Brussels sprouts, 2 heads celery and/or 450g (1lb) frozen peas and about 450g (1lb) canned or frozen sweetcorn, 4 good-sized grapefruit, small bunch white and black grapes, fruit, nuts.

Note

In view of the fact that so much can be prepared well beforehand for this meal, the list is not complete. You need to check on the recipes for stuffings, sauces except Sherry Custard Sauce, Christmas Pudding, Brandy Butter, Iced Christmas Pudding and Mince Pies and make an early shopping list.

Menu 52
Iced Christmas Pudding

Seafood Pancakes

For the batter
110g (4oz) plain flour
pinch salt
1 egg
scant 300ml (½pt) milk or milk and water
1tbspn oil

For frying
little oil or fat

For the filling and topping
50g (2oz) butter or margarine
50g (2oz) flour
600ml (1pt) milk
salt and pepper
100g (4oz) cooked smoked haddock
100g (4oz) cooked white fish
100g (4oz) peeled prawns
1tspn chopped parsley
1tspn chopped fennel

To garnish
lemon wedges

Boeuf à la Bourguignonne

For the marinade
1 medium onion
1 strip of lemon rind
1 bay leaf
1 sprig of thyme
150ml (¼pt) red Burgundy wine
1tbspn oil
salt and pepper

675g (1½lb) topside of beef
25g (1oz) flour
3 large onions
1 garlic clove
100g (4oz) streaky bacon cut in 1 thick slice
2tbspn oil
450ml (¾pt) beef stock
bouquet garni

To garnish
lemon wedges

Menu 53

Seafood Pancakes

Serves 6

Boeuf à la Bourguignonne
Parsley Potatoes — Macedoine of Vegetables

Fresh Fruit Salad

Seafood Pancakes

Blend together the ingredients for the pancake batter. Add the oil just before cooking—this helps to give crisp pancakes. Grease a pancake or frying pan with a very little oil or fat and heat. Pour in sufficient batter to give a paper-thin coating. Cook for approximately 1½-2 minutes. Turn or toss and cook on the second side. Repeat until all the batter is used; this makes 12 small or 10 larger pancakes.

Make a coating sauce with the butter or margarine, flour and milk. Season lightly. Pour half the sauce into a basin. Flake the fish, stir into the sauce, together with the prawns and herbs. Fill the pancakes with the fish mixture. Roll and put into an oven-proof serving dish. Top with the remaining sauce. Cover the dish and heat for 20 minutes above the centre of a moderate oven, 180-190°C, 350-375°F, Gas Mark 4-5. Garnish with lemon wedges.

Boeuf à la Bourguignonne

Peel and thinly slice the medium onion. Put into a casserole with the remaining marinade ingredients.

Cut the beef into neat fingers, approximately 2cm (¾in) in thickness. Put into the marinade; leave for 3 hours, turning once or twice. Lift the meat from the marinade. Add a little salt and pepper to the flour; coat the meat in this. Peel and thinly slice the 3 onions, peel the garlic, leave whole. Derind the bacon and cut into fingers about 1.5cm (½in) in width. Heat the 2tbspn oil and fry the onions, garlic, bacon and coated meat for 5-6 minutes, or until pale golden. Gradually blend in the stock; stir as the liquid comes to simmering point and thickens slightly. Strain the marinade into the other ingredients in the pan, add the bouquet garni and a little salt and pepper. Cover the pan and simmer very gently for 2 hours. Remove the bouquet garni and garlic. Serve with the lemon.

Method for cooking Parsley Potatoes, see Menu 7; Macedoine of Vegetables, see Menu 45.

Fresh Fruit Salad

Put the water into a saucepan, pare the top 'zest' from the orange, add to the water, together with the lemon juice and sugar; stir until the sugar has dissolved, then boil for several minutes. Allow to cool.

Prepare the fruits; divide into neat pieces, put into the serving dish; add the syrup at once to prevent the fruit discolouring. Serve very cold with cream.

To Make Sunday Easier

1 Cook and fill pancakes unless being frozen.
2 Cook Boeuf à la Bourguignonne; this improves with standing overnight in the refrigerator.
3 Prepare syrup for Fruit Salad.

Foods Required

675g (1½lb) topside of beef, 175g (6oz) smoked haddock and 175g (6oz) white fish (each should give 100g (4oz) when cooked), 100g (4oz) peeled prawns, 100g (4oz) butter or margarine, 150-300ml (¼-½pt) double or single cream, 1 egg, 900ml (1½pt) milk, 185g (7oz) plain flour, approximately 150ml (¼pt) oil (less if using fat for pancakes), 150ml (¼pt) red Burgundy wine, 100g (4oz) streaky bacon cut in 1 piece, 675g (1½lb) potatoes, ingredients for Macedoine of Vegetables (see Menu 45), 1 medium onion, 3 large onions, 1 garlic clove, parsley, fennel, bay leaf, thyme, herbs for bouquet garni, 2-3 lemons, mixed fruit for Fruit Salad.

Fresh Fruit Salad

For the syrup
300ml (½pt) water
1 orange
1tbspn lemon juice
100g (4oz) sugar

Basic fruits
1-2 dessert apples
1-2 bananas
few grapes
1-2 oranges
1-2 peaches and/or portion of fresh pineapple
1 dessert pear

Luxury fruits
kiwi fruit
strawberries
dessert cherries
fresh lychees
melon

Variation
Add a little kirsch or white wine.

To Freeze Ahead

Pancakes: cook and fill; freeze in a dish suitable for reheating and serving; put a little sauce under the pancakes as well as over them to prevent their drying when reheated. Use within 3 months.
Boeuf à la Bourguignonne can be frozen for up to 3 months. Do not over-cook meat before freezing.

Index